ANCIENT ISRAELITES

AND THEIR

NEIGHBORS

AN
ACTIVITY
GUIDE

MARIAN BROIDA

CHICAGO
REVIEW
PRESS

To Jeremy

Library of Congress Cataloging-in-Publication Data

Broida, Marian.
    Ancient Israelites and their neighbors : an activity guide / Marian
Broida.— 1st ed.
        p. cm.
        Summary: Examines the ancient cultures of the Israelites, the
Philistines, and the Phoenicians, focusing on art, architecture, food, clothing,
writing, history, religion, and work. Includes related activities.
        ISBN 1-55652-457-9 (alk. paper)
        1. Jews—History—953-586 B.C.—Juvenile literature. 2. Phoenicians—
History—Juvenile literature. 3. Philistines—History—Juvenile literature. 4.
Palestine—Civilization—History—Juvenile literature. [1. Jews—History—
953-586 B.C. 2. Phoenicians—History. 3. Philistines—History. 4. Palestine—
Civilization—History.] I. Title.
        DS121.B74 2003
        933'.02—dc21
                                                    2002155450

Front cover images (clockwise from upper right): *Phoenician Trade Ship*, Tail end of a sarcophagus, 5th–1st century B.C.E., National Archaeological Museum, Beirut, Lebanon. © Erich Lessing/Art Resource, NY; *Amulet*, Israel, 330–640 C.E., 3.5 x 5.5 in. The Jewish Museum, New York, Gift of Bernard and Tzila Weiss, 1994-664. Photo by John Parnell; Photograph of carvings on an Egyptian temple, Courtesy of Scott Noegel; *Camel Figurine*, Israel or Jordan, 1st–2nd century C.E., Mold-formed terracotta. 4 x 6 in. Gift of John Khayat. Photo by Richard Goodbody. The Jewish Museum, New York, NY, U.S.A. ©The Jewish Museum of New York/Art Resource, NY
Back cover image: ©Lawrence E. Stagner

Cover and interior design: Joan Sommers Design
Interior illustration: TJ Romero

© 2003 by Marian Broida
All rights reserved
First edition
Published by Chicago Review Press, Incorporated
814 North Franklin Street
Chicago, Illinois 60610
ISBN 1-55652-457-9
Printed in Singapore
5 4 3 2 1

CONTENTS

PART 1 ⊗ The Israelites 1

FOREWORD

The ancient Near East is as fascinating as it is vast. The more archaeologists dig up, the more questions we seem to have. The more questions we have, the more fun it becomes trying to answer them. This is especially true of the peoples who lived in the land once called Canaan, namely the Philistines, Phoenicians, and Israelites. Though the region is very small, roughly the size of Lake Michigan (!), it has fascinated people for hundreds of years.

This fascination is due, in part, to the huge impact that the Bible has had on world history and on the three great religious traditions of Judaism, Christianity, and Islam. In fact, you could even say that if we didn't have the Bible, the world we live in today would be very different. Certainly, three of the religions that are most familiar to us today would be different. Yet it isn't just the religions of these ancient peoples that interest us, but also their cultures—their languages, the way they built their homes, the way they traveled, the food they ate, the clothes they wore, the music they listened to, and of course, their many interesting stories.

Yet, speaking as a scholar of the ancient Near East, I can honestly say that getting to know the ancient Israelites, Philistines, and Phoenicians can be a difficult task, since there are so many things we don't know about them. The Bible, of course, and few other ancient texts do give us insights into their world, but even these records don't answer all of our questions. The discoveries of archaeologists also shed light on the world of these peoples, but archaeologists can provide only part of the picture. So getting to know these ancient peoples is sort of like trying to put together a big jigsaw puzzle that is missing a lot of its pieces.

What makes this book so great is that it gives us the largest and most important pieces to the puzzle and shows us how to have fun putting them together. Marian Broida introduces us firsthand to the Israelites, Philistines, and Phoenicians by showing us how to make food they might have eaten (yummy!) and how to construct models of their ancient homes, ships, musical instruments, and pottery. She even shows us how to write in the ancient Israelite alphabet, a script that hasn't been taught to kids for over 2,000 years.

What's more—and this your parents might like to know—is that this book informs us about these ancient cultures and their religions with historical accuracy and sensitivity to the complex issues surrounding the study of ancient Israel and its neighbors. This book, then, is interesting, informative, accurate, and—most of all—it is fun! So grab some paint, a little clay, and oh, yes, a bunch of newspaper for the mess, and let's get started!

Scott Noegel
Professor of Biblical and Ancient Near Eastern Studies
University of Washington

Time Line

This time line shows some of the important events in the lives of the ancient Israelites, Phoenicians, and Philistines. Like this book, it begins about 1200 B.C.E., when the Israelites were settling in the hills of Canaan, and ends about 600 years later, when many Israelites returned home from captivity in Babylonia.

From the Bible, you may know of the stories of Abraham, Isaac, and Jacob; their wives Sarah, Rebecca, Rachel, and Leah; and Moses, who led the Israelites out of slavery in Egypt. These stories took place before this time line begins.

All dates in this timeline are B.C.E.—before the year 1. Some people use the letters B.C. for such dates. Why do we say B.C.E.? You can read about it on page xvi.

The symbol ~ in front of a date means "about." ~ 1100 B.C.E. means "about 1,100 years before the year 1."

In ancient times, people didn't use the same kinds of systems for dates that we do today. Modern scholars have to estimate when some things occurred, and often they disagree. Don't be surprised if you find different dates elsewhere for some of these events.

Finally, these groups of people were very busy. This time line lists only a few of the most important events in their lives.

	BCE	1200	1150	1100	1050	1000	950	900

ISRAELITES

~1200 Israelites begin settling in hill country of Canaan

~1200–1020 Period of Judges

~1020–928 Period of United Monarchy

~1020–1004 First king, Saul, rules Israel

~1004–965 David rules

~928–721 Period of Divided Kingdom

~928–907 Jeroboam I rules Israel

~928–911 Rehoboam rules Judah

~965–928 Solomon rules

~950 Solomon builds Temple

PHOENICIANS

~1100 Story of Wen-Amun written down

~1000 Inscription on coffin of Ahiram of Byblos

~969–936 Hiram I rules Tyre

PHILISTINES

1175 Philistines and other Sea Peoples attack Egypt

~1174 Philistines and other Sea Peoples settle in Canaan

~1100–965 Wars with Israelites

~961 David of Israel stops Philistine expansion

850	800	750	700	650	600	550	500

~841 Jehu of Israel swears loyalty to Assyria

727–698 Hezekiah rules Judah

721 Assyria destroys Samaria and exiles northern Israelites

~640 Assyria withdraws from Canaan

612 Babylonia conquers Assyria

~640–605 Egypt dominates Canaan

597 Babylonians temporarily occupy Judah

701 Assyria destroys cities in Judah; Hezekiah defends Jerusalem

587 Babylonia conquers Jerusalem

~871–852 Ahab rules Israel

640–609 Josiah rules Judah

587–538 Babylonian Exile

~622 Josiah discovers scroll in temple

538 Cyrus II of Persia defeats Babylonia; lets Israelites go home

~814 Elissa establishes colony of Carthage

644 Assyria attacks Phoenicia for the last time

~550 General from Carthage defeats Greeks in Sicily

738 Assyria invades Phoenicia

~625–604 Phoenicia under Egyptian control

701 King Luli flees Tyre as Assyrians attack

604 Babylonia demands tribute from Phoenicia

677 Assyria destroys Sidon

671 Tyre surrenders to Assyria

601–597 Tyre and Sidon ally with Judah and others against Babylonia

662 After rebelling, Tyre surrenders to Assyria again

585–572 Babylonia lays siege to Tyre

734–701 Multiple Assyrian invasions and Philistine rebellions

604–603 King Nebuchadnezzar II of Babylonia conquers Philistine cities; end of Philistine culture

716 Philistines begin to prosper under Assyrian control

676–667 King Ikuasu (Achish) rules Ekron

~640 Assyrians withdraw from land of Philistines

640–605 Egypt dominates Canaan

Introduction

About 3,200 years ago, huge changes occurred in lands around the eastern Mediterranean Sea. Mighty empires buckled as shiploads of invaders attacked their coasts. New people entered ancient lands, among them the land of *Canaan* (KAY-nan or Ke-NA-an) in western Asia. Philistines (FILL-iss-teens) settled on Canaan's southern coast, while Israelites (IZ-ray-e-lites) built small villages on its sparsely settled hills. Canaanites called the Phoenicians (fo-NEE-shuns) took advantage of the weakening empires and began to create their own. These three ancient groups—the Israelites, Phoenicians, and Philistines—shared the land once called Canaan during a time known as the Iron Age. Their cultures are described in this book.

Where Was the Land of Canaan?

From synagogue or church, you may think of Canaan as the home of the ancient Israelite people—a country perhaps the size of modern Israel and the Palestinian territories combined. But ancient writings on stone or clay give a different meaning to the name Canaan. In these inscriptions, ancient Canaan was much bigger than modern Israel. It included Lebanon to the north, parts of modern Syria and Jordan, and Israel and the Palestinian territories.

Ancient Canaan was a region, not a country. Its inhabitants included the Jebusites (JEB-yoo-sites), Horvites, Amorites, and others. We don't know the names of all these groups. The Bible sometimes just calls them Canaanites.

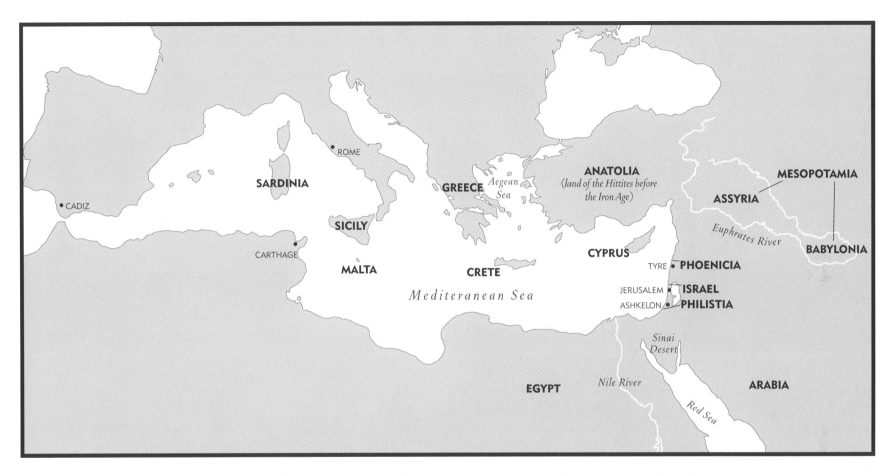

The Mediterranean Sea during the Iron Age: places mentioned in this book

In modern Jerusalem, an ancient tower catches the sun. It's part of a structure called the Citadel, first erected by King Herod about 2,000 years ago and rebuilt several times since. Even the oldest parts of the Citadel were built long after the events in this book. Courtesy of Scott Noegel.

What Is This Book About?

This book is about how the Israelites, Phoenicians, and Philistines lived their daily lives in the land they shared. Reading it, you'll learn to do many things, such as:

- serve a meal ancient Israelite style
- build a model Phoenician ship
- write messages in ancient alphabets
- fashion Israelite, Phoenician, and Philistine costumes and headdresses
- create a model Philistine lyre (a stringed musical instrument)
- shape a Phoenician-style mask
- mold a Philistine bird-shaped bowl
- make grape juice with your feet

You'll learn about examples of ancient writing—crumbling silver scrolls engraved with a blessing like one still used today, and a mysterious inscription perhaps written by a long-dead Philistine. You'll learn how the Israelites turned hillsides into farms growing grain and fruit trees, and how bold Phoenician sailors risked their lives traveling to far-off lands. You'll also learn about less-pleasant subjects such as captivity, child sacrifice, and war.

What Time Period Does This Book Cover?

This book covers events between the years 1200 B.C.E. and 538 B.C.E., with occasional side trips to periods before and after.

Have you ever seen the letters B.C.E. after a date? They stand for "Before the Common Era"—a fancy way of saying "before the year 1." (See "Telling Time" page xvi.) The first date, 1200 B.C.E., occurred 1,200 years before the year 1 (or about 3,200 years ago). The second date, 538 B.C.E., occurred only 538 years before the year 1. You'll notice the bigger date happened longer ago.

The dates 1200 B.C.E. and 538 B.C.E. were picked for reasons. 1200 B.C.E. marked the entry of the Philistines and Israelites into Canaan. 538 B.C.E. marked another important date—the time the Persian King Cyrus II (SIGH-russ the second) allowed the people of Jerusalem, captured in war, to return to their land. Obviously, there's a story there and many stories in between. You'll learn some of those stories in this book.

The Iron Age

There's another way to name this book's time period: the Iron Age. That's the period when people used iron to make knives, swords, and other tools and weapons. Scholars like to name periods in ancient history after the material used to make tools. Just before the Iron Age was the Bronze Age, and before that were the Copper Age and the Stone Age.

In reality, things weren't quite this simple, because people didn't change their ways all at once. People in the Iron Age still made many tools of bronze and even stone—but they knew how to make iron tools, too. Earlier, in the Bronze Age, people made a few objects out of iron, but not well. Their brittle knives and swords shattered too easily.

Telling Time

Most books use the letters B.C. for dates occurring before the year 1. Why does this book use the letters B.C.E.?

The letters B.C. stand for a religious phrase—"Before Christ." Christians believe that Jesus, also called Christ, was born around the year 1—a religious event. Some people would rather use B.C.E. because it stands for a non-religious phrase, "Before the Common Era." If you prefer B.C., just say those letters in your head when you see B.C.E.

People who use B.C. for dates before the year 1 usually use A.D. for dates occurring after the year 1: for example, 800 A.D. (800 years after the year 1). But A.D., like B.C., is a religious term, standing for "Anno Domini," Latin for "the year of our Lord." "Our Lord" refers to Jesus. Instead of A.D., some people say C.E., which stands for the Common Era.

Canaan Transformed

During the Late Bronze Age, just before the Israelites and Philistines appeared, Canaan was a land of many small city-states—walled cities ruled by kings who also controlled the surrounding countryside. Their inhabitants—the Canaanites—farmed, made fine jewelry and purple dye, traded extensively, and worshipped gods and goddesses. Around Canaan loomed much larger civilizations, including Egypt and Mesopotamia (which includes Assyria and Babylonia). The larger civilizations sought to control the small kingdoms of Canaan, and demanded tribute (payment of precious goods) and loyalty—or else.

With the Iron Age came a new way of life. The Philistines moved into cities in the coastal plains, bringing with them traditions from across the sea. The Israelites settled in the Canaanite hills, eventually forming their own united monarchy (kingdom). Some Canaanites continued to live as they always had, but their influence decreased. Only in the north, among the Phoenicians, did Canaanite heritage truly live on.

One thing didn't change during the Iron Age: the meddling of the larger civilizations. During the Iron Age, Assyria, Egypt, and Babylonia at different times controlled the people in this book: the Phoenicians, Philistines, and Israelites.

The Phoenicians

The Phoenicians lived mostly in northern Canaan, in an area called Lebanon. (Today, a country bearing that name occupies nearly the same location.) They inhabited the famous ancient cities of Tyre (TIRE), Byblos (BIB-los), and Sidon (SIGH-don). Living on the coast, they sailed the sea in well-built ships and became famous navigators, sailors, and traders. They established colonies around the Mediterranean Sea and formed a trading empire that lasted long after the period covered by this book.

— ⊗ —

The Peoples, Yes

Do you think it's odd to see the word "people" with an "s" after it? That's because a "people" can mean all those sharing the same religion, government, or culture—for example, the American people, or the Israelite people. Among the Sea Peoples, there were several different cultural groups.

Carvings on an Egyptian temple show Philistine prisoners, captured in a long-ago battle in Egypt a few years before the Philistines entered Canaan. Courtesy of Scott Noegel.

The Philistines

The Philistines came to Canaan by way of the Mediterranean Sea. Scholars call them, and other related groups, the "Sea Peoples." Before arriving in Canaan, the Sea Peoples battled the Egyptians as well as other peoples north of Canaan. In Canaan, they settled on the southern coast in large, impressive cities. At first the Israelites' enemies, they later lived next to them in relative peace.

Much about the Sea Peoples—such as the exact location of their homeland—remains mysterious. You'll read about these mysteries—and some possible answers—in this book.

The Israelites

The Israelites are best known to us by the Hebrew Bible, also called the Old Testament. The Bible tells the stirring story of their flight from Egypt, and the covenant (treaty or agreement) they made with God at Mount Sinai (SIGH-nigh) on the way to Canaan. Their first settlements in Canaan were small and crude. As the Israelites grew in power, they developed a kingdom. Their second king, David, conquered Jerusalem and made it his capital.

After King David's son Solomon died, the Israelite kingdom split in two, with Israel to the north and Judah to the south. In this book, we usually call the inhabitants of both kingdoms Israelites.

The Assyrians demolished Israel, but not Judah, in 721 B.C.E. Judah lasted until the Babylonians destroyed Jerusalem in 587 B.C.E. Many of Jerusalem's people returned home from captivity in Babylonia about 50 years later—the endpoint of this book.

How Do We Know What We Know?

Thousands of years have passed since the Israelites, Philistines, and Phoenicians planted crops, built their homes, and baked their bread. It's amazing that we know anything at all about their lives. In fact, we have several fine sources: the Bible, other ancient writings, and archaeology.

Containing the Israelites' sacred stories, history, and law, the Hebrew Bible tells us much about daily life during the Iron Age. It can't answer all our questions—it's a religious book, after all, not a cookbook, building manual, or fashion magazine. Also, much of it was written down long after the time periods it talks about, leading scholars to wonder if the customs it describes come from Iron Age times or later. They also wonder if the Israelites accurately described their enemies—the Philistines, for example.

Other writings help illuminate the past. Egyptian kings and others ordered carvings boasting of their conquests in Canaan. Later Greek and Roman historians described (not always accurately) Iron Age peoples and events. The Iron Age Phoenicians and Israelites themselves left a few prayers engraved on tombs, letters scrawled on pottery, or labels stamped on storage jars. Unlike writings on softer materials, these did not rot away.

There's a third important source of information: archaeology, the study of ancient objects. People called archaeologists dig up objects, called artifacts, from buried cities and homes. Only certain objects are likely to have

Secrets in a Name

For many centuries, Westerners wondered about the exact locations of many places named in the Bible. For example, the Bible mentioned a city called Shiloh—but where was it exactly? No one knew.

In the mid-1800s, two men, Robinson and Smith, decided to track down some of the places named in the Bible. They did something no Westerner had ever done: they compared biblical place-names with the place-names used by people living in the area.

At the time they tried this—a century before the state of Israel was founded—the southern part of ancient Canaan was known as Palestine, under Turkish control, and mostly populated by Arabs. By talking to Arab residents, Robinson and Smith found many similarities between biblical and modern names—even after 2,000 years! Place-names change over time, of course, so the names weren't exact matches—but they were close enough to be useful. The men determined that Shiloh, for example, probably existed, millennia earlier, in a place the Arabs called Seilun.

Since then, archaeologists have confirmed many of Robinson's and Smith's conclusions. Never mind that 2,000 years had passed—the ancient Israelite names lived on.

survived until our time—mainly hard things like bronze bracelets, clay jugs, stone walls, and some of the writings mentioned earlier.

Archaeologists are like detectives—they figure out how people lived from the clues these people leave behind. Bracelets tell them a bit about the fashion of the day. Charred wheat grains give evidence of what people ate. The customs of modern people in the region sometimes offer clues as well.

By themselves, these pieces of information give only tidbits of data. Scholars must interpret them to tell us if a set of ruins might have been a house, a temple, or a workshop. Often, scholars differ in their interpretations. Still, by combining archaeology, the Bible, and other writings, they are painting a picture of ancient life that grows more detailed, rich, and colorful every day.

The Region Today

As you probably know, the land once called Canaan is today mired in conflict. Decades of bloodshed have shadowed the lives of its modern-day inhabitants, including Israelis, Palestinians, and Lebanese. Efforts at peacemaking have not always succeeded. A long period of bloodshed within Lebanon ended a decade or so ago, but to the south, conflicts between Israelis and Palestinians persist.

Keep in mind that the events in this book happened thousands of years in the past. Since then, enormous changes have affected the region and the wider world: large-scale migration of Arabs to the region, the development of Christianity and Islam, the rise and collapse of the Turkish empire, two world wars, French and British control of the area, the founding of the modern state of Israel, peace accords, protests, and global terrorism—just to name a few.

Still, one message holds true, in ancient times as today. In every period of history, different peoples have shared the land once called Canaan. Each people had its own triumphs and tragedies, outlook and customs, and—always—humanity. All of these peoples deserve to have their stories known.

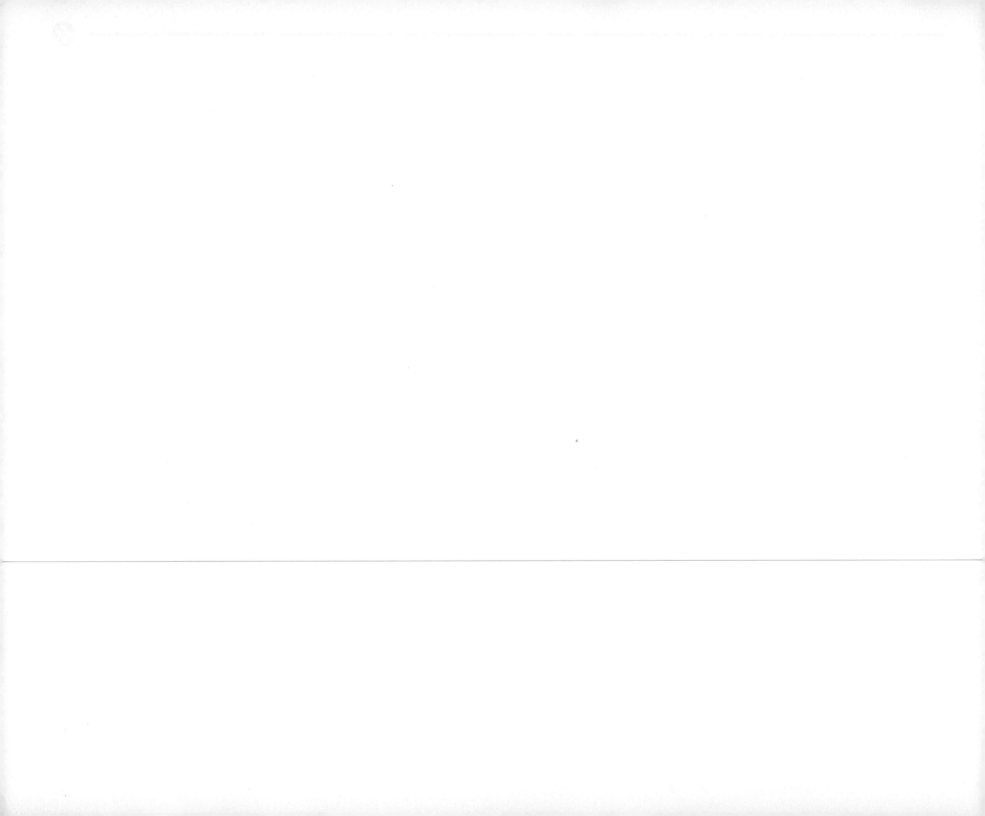

PART 1

THE ISRAELITES

Israel, Phoenicia, and Philistia during the Iron Age. The area called "Judah" on the map was part of Israel until about 928 B.C.E.

Israelite History

Around 1200 B.C.E., Canaan was part of a world in turmoil. All the great civilizations of the region were in flux. For hundreds of years, Egypt had held power over the cities of Canaan, but now its hold was weakening. Egypt's chief rivals, the Hittites, would soon fall to attackers. Suddenly, no great power ruled the region. Canaan was due for an enormous change.

Around this time, an obscure people began to settle in Canaan's central hills. So poor were their settlements, so crude their tools, that no one could have imagined the influence they would have. Yet these obscure people, the Israelites, left a legacy unlike any other in the world. Instead of riches, knowledge, or fine art, their legacy was a religious one. Thousands of years later, people across the world would know about the Israelites' God.

Be aware that many stories can be told about the Israelites—historians, archaeologists, and people of different faiths tell their stories differently. At times they disagree.

What the Bible Tells Us

Ruins at Hazor.
Courtesy of Scott Noegel.

The Hebrew Bible traces the Israelites' beginnings to seven people: Abraham, Isaac, and Jacob; Sarah, Rebecca, Rachel, and Leah.

In the Bible, Abraham and his wife Sarah followed God's command to leave their home in Mesopotamia for Canaan. There, Sarah bore Isaac, who married Rebecca. Their son Jacob married Rachel and Leah, and fathered a daughter and 12 sons. An angel wrestled with Jacob and gave him a new name: Israel. Jacob's children became the "children of Israel"—the term the Bible uses for the Israelites.

Jacob's sons had personal problems, to say the least. Nine of them sold their brother Joseph, Jacob's favorite, to slave traders. The slave traders took Joseph to Egypt. There, Joseph's adventures included slavery, prison, and a rise to great power. Later, his family ended up in Egypt as well. (The story in the Bible is quite exciting—you might want to read it!) In time, according to the Bible, Jacob's descendants became slaves to the Egyptian king, until an Israelite named Moses (who was raised as an Egyptian prince) guided them to freedom. Moses led the Israelites to Mount Sinai, where they made a covenant with God and received the Ten Commandments. After Moses' death and 40 years wandering in the desert, they settled in Canaan—a land, says the Bible, flowing with milk and honey.

From the northern city of Dan to the southern town of Beer-Sheba (bare-SHEE-ba), the Israelites came to occupy most of southern Canaan—the location of the modern state of Israel. To their east lay the Jordan River. To their south lay desert. To their north was Lebanon, home of the Phoenicians. The Philistines lived in the fertile fields to the west, by the sea. Like modern Israelis, the ancient Israelites called their land Israel.

The Bible says the Israelites' first leaders were judges (actually military leaders), with names like Deborah, Gideon (GID-ee-un), and Samuel. Then, when battles broke out between the Philistines and Israelites, the Israelites demanded a king. Their first king, Saul, died in shame after losing a battle. But their next king, David, defeated the Philistines and made Jerusalem his capital. There, David's son, King Solomon, built God a mighty temple from fragrant Phoenician cedar and costly stone.

The Bible says that Solomon reigned over an immense area, from the Euphrates (yoo-FRAY-teez) River in Mesopotamia to Egypt's border. Some archaeologists believe his realm was really much smaller. According to the Bible, the reigns of King David and King Solomon included the Israelites' most powerful years. Scholars call their reigns—and King Saul's—the "United

The Tribes of Israel

According to the Bible, the Israelites were organized into tribes named for 11 of Jacob's sons and two of Joseph's. The tribes included Judah, Benjamin, and Levi. Twelve of the tribes—all except Levi—had their own territories in Canaan. The Bible tells us that the tribe of Levi lived in the other tribes' territories, serving their religious needs.

Three Great Religions

From the ancient Israelites' religion grew three others, each with its own holy book: Judaism, practiced by Jews; Christianity, practiced by Christians; and Islam, practiced by Muslims.

Both Jews and Muslims claim descent from Abraham (Ibrahim in Arabic) through his two sons Isaac and Ishmael. The Jews claim Isaac as their forefather, and the Muslims claim Ishmael. The Muslim holy book, the Quran (kur-AN), names Moses as a prophet—the same Moses who guided the Israelites to Canaan in the Hebrew Bible.

Many Christians consider themselves the spiritual descendants of the Jews. They have added their own holy text, called the New Testament, to the Hebrew Bible, which they call the Old Testament.

Of course, all these religions are different. Muslims follow the teachings of their most important prophet, Muhammad (muh-HAM-mad). Christians follow the teachings of Jesus. The Hebrew Bible was written before either Jesus or Muhammad lived.

Underneath the differences, the religions have much in common. Religious Jews, Christians, and Muslims all worship one God.

Monarchy." It lasted until King Solomon's death, when the kingdom split into two—one part ruled by Solomon's son, and the other by a man named Jeroboam I (jer-o-BOE-am the first), who was chosen by the northern Israelites to be their king.

The northern kingdom, called Israel, and the southern kingdom, called Judah, existed side by side for several hundred years, each ruled by its own king. Scholars call this period of history "the Divided Kingdom."

Again and again, Assyrian armies invaded the region during this period, burning cities that denied them tribute. Eventually Assyria conquered the northern kingdom of Israel. Historians know this happened in 721 B.C.E.

The Assyrians attacked Judah too, and set its cities aflame. But they didn't destroy Jerusalem. Judah's King Hezekiah (heh-zeh-KIE-a) stripped the gold from the Temple's doors to pay the tribute the Assyrians demanded. Even so, the Assyrians planned to destroy the city. As the Bible tells it, an angel saved Jerusalem, and slayed the Assyrian soldiers camped outside its walls. We hear no more of the Assyrians in the Bible after that.

All was not quiet for long, however. An Egyptian pharaoh killed Josiah (jo-ZIE-ah),

This ancient wall from the city of Dan shows carefully prepared stones. Courtesy of Scott Noegel.

Archaeology and the Bible

For more than a century, archaeologists have dug in the land once called Canaan for two different reasons. Some have sought to prove that the Bible is true. Others—regardless of their religions—have simply sought to know how the ancient inhabitants lived.

Archaeology—the study of ancient objects—can shed light on the Israelites' lives. Sometimes it can even show that events in the Bible really occurred. But it can't prove or disprove anything the Bible says about God, miracles, or many other spiritual matters. Believing in God or miracles is a matter of faith.

another king of Judah. Then the Babylonian king Nebuchadnezzar II (ne-bu-khad-NEZ-zar the second) burned Jerusalem, destroyed its Temple, and brought many of its people into Babylonia as captives. (Historians call this the "Babylonian Exile," dating it to 587 B.C.E.) The people of Judah lived in Babylon until Cyrus II of Persia conquered the Babylonians and let them return home. Historians know this happened in 538 B.C.E.—the end point of this book.

Archaeologists have been digging up the Israelites' past since the end of the 1800s, when the land was known as Palestine and was inhabited mainly by Arabs. Since 1948, when Israel became a state, excavations have increased.

Archaeologists believe they've found evidence of the first Israelite settlements: many ancient villages—groups of three to eight houses—built around 1200 B.C.E. in the central hills. Coarse, simple pottery and the lack of luxuries showed that the settlers' lives were hard and poor. As time went on, some of these tiny settlements grew, while others were abandoned.

In later periods, buildings and gateways of carefully hewn stone appeared. Most scholars agree that only an organized kingdom would have had funds for this kind of construction. Some of these buildings may date from the United Monarchy, perhaps from King Solomon's time.

During the Divided Kingdom, signs of wealth increased. Samaria, ancient capital of the northern kingdom, contained hoards of carved Phoenician ivories, just as the Bible describes. Some Israelite houses held

Did King David Really Live?

Archaeologists have sometimes questioned the Bible's historical accuracy. For example, archaeologists have found no trace of the Israelites' flight from Egypt, leading some to wonder if it ever took place, or if it involved fewer people than the Bible suggests.

A few individuals even questioned whether King David really lived. According to the Bible, David conquered Jerusalem and founded a dynasty (a family of kings) that ruled in Judah for years. If David was as famous and powerful as the Bible suggests, they said archaeologists would have surely found his name in writings outside the Bible. But no one ever had.

All this changed on July 21, 1993, when archaeologists discovered an inscription on a broken piece of stone in the Israelite city of Dan. In the inscription, an Israelite enemy bragged of besting "a king of Israel" and mentioned "the House of David."

This inscription confirmed that King David had indeed once ruled Israel—a discovery that excited scholars worldwide. Perhaps, in time, archaeologists will uncover traces of the Israelites' flight from Egypt as well—who knows?

Philistine, Phoenician, and other imported pottery; glass beads; and decorated containers for homemade cosmetics. Some towns and cities even had gutters for collecting rainwater! Still, many homes were humble, with few luxuries.

Archaeologists have also found many writings jotted on broken pottery from the Divided Kingdom period. This shows that people could read. Carved on a piece of stone called a seal (see page 27) was the name of a servant of King Jeroboam—probably Jeroboam II from the northern kingdom of Israel.

Records of violence exist, too. King Sennacherib (sen-na-KHE-rib) of Assyria displayed wall carvings showing his soldiers destroying Lachish (la-KHEESH), an important city in Judah, in 701 B.C.E. In the pictures, Assyrians are running battering rams (thick poles) up a huge ramp to pound the city walls. Archaeologists found the remains of the ramp in Lachish, along with stones the Assyrians flung into the city.

In Jerusalem, archaeologists found sad evidence of the Babylonians' attack: rooms full of burned objects and arrowheads from both sides—Judah and Babylonia. Trying to get every possible bit of evidence, archaeologists even examined dried-up feces (poop) in Jerusalem toilets. Their tests showed that the people of Jerusalem were probably eating weeds to survive.

In Judah archaeologists also found pottery and jewelry from the time of the Babylonian exile. These show that some Israelites stayed behind.

Hezekiah's Tunnel

The Bible describes a tunnel that King Hezekiah ordered to protect the city during a siege. Through this tunnel, the people of Jerusalem could reach a spring outside the city's walls, even when enemy soldiers surrounded the city. In 1880 C.E., a young Arab man lost his balance inside this tunnel and spotted an inscription carved on the moist rock. Translated, it told how two teams of laborers finished the tunnel by digging toward each other from either end. When they heard each other's voices, the inscription said, "the quarrymen hewed, each man toward his fellow, axe against axe," until the tunnel was done.

Israelite Architecture

The Israelites built most of their houses by stacking rough stones and mud bricks into walls and then using mud to hold the walls together. Branches, wood beams, and brush topped with more mud formed the roofs.

Floors were usually hard-beaten earth, but some rooms were cobbled (covered with small stones). Some scholars think that these cobblestone rooms may have housed donkeys, cows, goats, or sheep. In winter, the animals' bodies would help warm the house, while their dung (dried poop scooped up from the cobblestone floors) fueled the cooking fire.

A typical house was 10 to 13 yards long (9 to 12 m) and 8 to 11 yards (7 to 10 m) wide. Many of these houses had a second story constructed of wood or mud bricks. Is your home bigger or smaller?

Pillared Houses

Archaeologists have two different names for typical Israelite houses. They call them "pillared houses" because pillars replaced one or two inside walls. They also call them "four-room houses," because most had four main rooms on the ground floor. (See the diagram at left for common floor plans.) Similar houses also existed outside of Israelite territory—for example, in Iron Age settlements across the Jordan River.

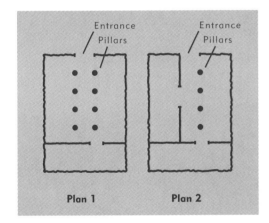

These are two possible plans for the ground floor of a four-room house, seen from above. The family might use one or two rooms for storage, and the others (including the courtyard) for many purposes. If there was a second floor, people might sleep there, or on the roof.

The middle room in most pillared houses, called a courtyard, opened to the sky. Families could cook, work, or eat there in nice weather.

Living in a Pillared House

Imagine you are visiting an Iron Age pillared house. The first thing you might notice would be darkness. Only a few small windows, high up, let in light.

You would smell burning dung, leather, smoke, cooking odors, the olive oil used in lamps, and perhaps animals living inside.

You would notice one or two rooms crammed with large clay storage jars of grain, oil, dried fruit, or wine. Because they didn't have supermarkets, people had to store half a year's supply of food at a time. Sometimes people stored grain in plaster-lined pits dug into the floor.

Unless the family was fairly rich, you would see little furniture. But in the courtyard you would see a loom for weaving cloth, grindstones for crushing grain, and perhaps a dome-shaped oven or a hearth.

If the house had a second floor, you'd have to go outside to climb the stairs, or clamber up a ladder inside. Upstairs you might see

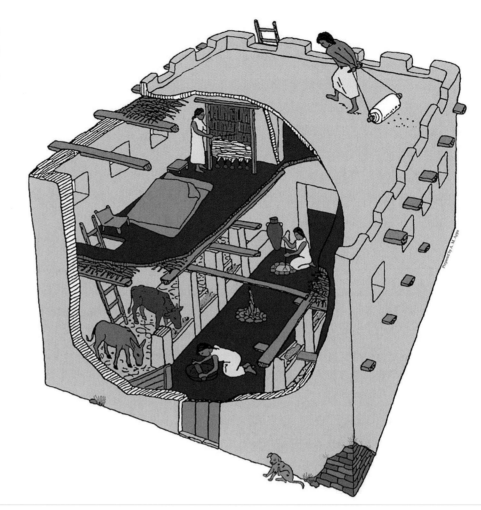

This drawing shows a typical Israelite pillared house from the early Iron Age, with stables, storage, food processing, and a cistern on the ground floor to hold water. The upper story is for sleeping, dining, and entertaining. A man with a roof roller keeps the mud roof intact to prevent leaks. Inside, women are weaving on a loom and grinding grain into flour. © Lawrence E. Stager.

ACTIVITY

Model Pillared House

If you like details, you'll love this project. See pages 10 and 13 for ideas for furniture ideas.

Materials

Newspaper or other table protection

Lidless cardboard box, 8 to 10 inches (20 to 25 cm) per side, about 4 inches (10 cm) tall

Acrylic or tempera paint, in brown, tan, or white

Paintbrushes

Jar of water

Pencil

Scissors

Thin, white posterboard, at least 14 by 20 inches (35 x 50 cm)

Ruler or tape measure

Glue or double-stick tape

Tape

1 piece coarse sandpaper for dirt floor

Corrugated cardboard, 10 by 10 inches (25 x 25 cm) or smaller

Duct tape

1 cup small pebbles, about ¼ inch (6 mm) in diameter

Directions

Spread out the newspaper on the table. Paint the box (except the floor) brown, tan, or white, inside and out.

While the paint dries, choose a plan from page 9 for the ground floor. Do you want pillars around the courtyard? Will one room hold animals? You can also make some of the furnishings during this time.

Mark your walls on the floor with pencil. Don't forget to mark doorways.

Cut a doorway in one narrow end of the box.

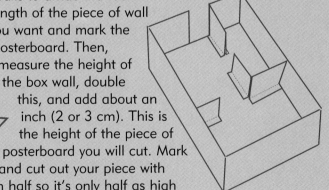

Make the walls to divide the rooms. Measure the length of the piece of wall you want and mark the posterboard. Then, measure the height of the box wall, double this, and add about an inch (2 or 3 cm). This is the height of the piece of posterboard you will cut. Mark it and cut out your piece with scissors. Fold in half so it's only half as high (the length stays the same). Stand the wall up in the house with the fold at the top. It should be a little too tall. Fold out the extra at the bottom, splaying out the two edges so it stands up. Glue or tape the two inner sides of the wall together, then tape the two splayed edges down in the box. Strengthen the wall by taping it to the box walls.

To make a pillar, cut a piece of posterboard about 3 inches (8 cm) wide and about ½ inch (1 cm) longer than the height of the wall. Roll into a tube the long way. Put 2 to 3 pieces of tape around the tube. In one end, make four cuts about ½ inch (1 cm) long. Splay out the cut pieces and tape them to the floor.

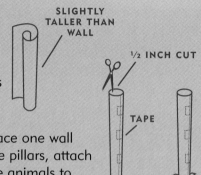

SLIGHTLY TALLER THAN WALL

½ INCH CUT

TAPE

If you want to make a room for animals, replace one wall with pillars. In between the pillars, attach walls low enough for the animals to look over.

Make dirt floors. Cut out pieces of sandpaper to fit inside the rooms and glue them on the box floor, rough side up. Cut small pieces to fit between and around any pillars. (Tape and glue don't stick well to the sandpaper surface, so be sure to attach the walls before putting down the floor.)

For a cobbled floor, cut a piece of corrugated cardboard to fit inside the animal's room. Glue duct tape sticky-side up onto one side of the cardboard. Cover the duct tape with pebbles, pressing down firmly. Glue the cardboard onto the box floor.

SANDPAPER PIECES

GLUE DUCT TAPE STICKY SIDE UP

Conquered Cities

Like other peoples of their time, the Israelites not only built cities, they also conquered them. King David captured the city of Jerusalem from people called the Jebusites. Often, after conquering a city, the Israelites built new walls, gates, and buildings on top of the old ones.

Think of the pain and bloodshed involved in conquering a city where others live. Would the world accept this behavior today?

A(TIVITY

Making Furniture

Furnish your model house using Sculpey or other clay, fabric scraps, pipe cleaners, and twine. You can also add miniature people and possibly toy animals. Adult supervision recommended when baking the clay.

Materials

Bakeable clay, such as Sculpey
Pipe cleaners
Twine
Felt and fabric scraps

Directions

Shape clay into a dome-shaped oven, grindstones, cooking pots and bowls, and larger storage jars for food. Follow directions on the package for baking. Wash your hands after using bakeable clay. Weave baskets for storing food or clothes from pipe cleaners and twine. Use scraps of felt or fabric for sleeping mats.

FOOD STORAGE JAR

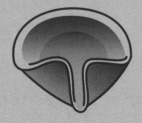

GRINDSTONES

OVEN

OIL LAMP

rolled-up sleeping mats, along with pegs, baskets, or boxes for clothes. A wealthy family might have a wooden bed, couch, table, and chairs inlaid with intricate ivory panels from Phoenicia.

Villages and Towns

The earliest Israelites lived in villages. In some villages, jumbles of houses faced every which way, but in others, all the houses faced the middle of a circle. For defense, the houses were sometimes connected, with their back walls forming a ring. A gap in the ring let people out to farm their fields.

In many early villages, nearly everyone was related. As the children grew up, the young men stayed and built their own houses. The young women—usually teenagers—often married boys or men from outside the village and moved to their husbands' homes. If the village kept growing, it might become a town—a larger village with a stronger defensive wall. In time the town might even become a city.

Ruins of the ancient city of Hazor show chambers opening off each side of the gates. The gate doors are missing. Only the foundations of the walls remain. Courtesy of Scott Noegel.

14

The City Gates

Ancient Israelites used rooms inside the city gates to conduct business. In the Bible, a man named Boaz (BOE-az) asked 10 city elders to sit in the gates to witness a meeting between himself and another man. Boaz needed the man's permission in order to marry a widow named Ruth. The man sealed his agreement following Israelite custom—he took off his sandal in front of the witnesses and handed it to Boaz. Once the agreement was sealed, Boaz and Ruth could marry. Their great-grandson was King David.

Cities

The biggest Israelite cities, Jerusalem and Samaria, would seem tiny to us today. At their largest, they probably held 18,000 to 20,000 people. Compare that to the size of modern cities in the United States like Washington, D.C., or Detroit, with about 500,000 inhabitants each—or New York City, with more than 7 million (7,000,000). But to an Israelite villager, their cities must have seemed grand indeed. Some of them even had paved streets. They also had larger buildings with neatly shaped stones, stronger walls, and elaborate gates.

City walls had gates to let people in and out. Each morning, gatekeepers opened the heavy doors. Each evening, they closed them for protection. But city gates were more than doors. Just inside the doors, a row of rooms opened off each side. Each room had built-in benches where people could sit.

Israelite Clothing

The clothing of the ancient Israelites is now dust, like the Israelites themselves. In the climate of Canaan, only hard objects have endured: hoop-shaped earrings, rings for fingers and toes, bronze hair curlers, and colored eye paint that Israelite women ground on stone plates. Sometimes archaeologists have even found ancient bronze safety pins called fibulas (FIB-you-luhs) lying among a skeleton's bones. But the garments the fibulas once fastened have vanished.

Without real clothing, how do we know what ancient Israelites wore? The Bible tells us little, and the Israelites themselves made few pictures.

Some of the best sources come from the Assyrians, the Israelites' ancient enemies. Boastful Assyrian kings ordered carvings of Israelites offering tribute or fleeing from their soldiers. Little did they know we'd be using them to see how the Israelites dressed.

Pictures from the Past

Decorating King Sennacherib's palace in Assyria were carvings of an attack on Lachish, a city in Judah, in 701 B.C.E. The pictures—now in the British Museum—show the Israelites marching barefoot from their city or kneeling before their captors.

An Assyrian carving shows an Israelite family leaving the city of Lachish, forced out by Assyrian soldiers. © The British Museum.

In these pictures, women wear long, straight, sleeveless dresses. Headscarves trail down their backs. Some of the men wear knee-length garments with short sleeves and fringed sashes. Turbans cover their heads, with a fringed end dangling over one ear. The men have short curly hair. Some have beards but not mustaches; others are clean-shaven. Older children dress exactly like their parents. Younger children wear simple, straight, ankle-length gowns or nothing at all.

About 140 years earlier, the Assyrian king Shalmaneser III (shal-man-ESS-er the third) had his own set of carvings made. These show King Jehu (YAY-hoo) of the northern kingdom of Israel paying him tribute. The Israelite king and his servants (probably high officials) wear full beards and floppy caps, like old-fashioned nightcaps, over long hair. Their short-sleeved robes end with a fringed hem just above the ankle. Over their robes, the servants wear long open coats with decorated borders. Their shoes have turned-up toes.

Compared to the pictures from Lachish, these carvings show a very different style of dress. Clothing probably differed between north and south, and between rich and poor. Fashions probably changed over time as well.

Israelite boys follow their father with the family's belongings as they flee Lachish. This is a carving from the palace of Sennacherib, an Assyrian king.
© The British Museum.

ACTIVITY

Boy's Tunic, Kilt, and Belt

You can dress like a boy from Lachish circa 701 B.C.E. Finish your costume with a turban (page 20), armbands (see page 22), sandals, and perhaps a cylinder seal around your neck (see page 28).

Materials

Plain short-sleeved T-shirt (without buttons) that hangs at least halfway down your thighs

Plain piece of cloth about 8 inches (20 cm) wide and long enough to go 1½ times or more around your waist

Safety pins

Strip of cloth about 4 inches (10 cm) wide and about 10 feet (3 m) long (You can safety-pin shorter pieces end-to-end.)

Scissors

Directions

Put on the T-shirt. (You can wear shorts underneath.) Wrap the 8-inch (20-cm) wide piece of cloth around your waist over the shirt, and pin in place. Let several inches (5 to 7 cm) of shirt show underneath. Now take the 10-foot (3-m) strip of cloth and cut long, skinny fringes along one of the narrower ends. Starting with the other uncut end, wrap it around and around your waist to hold the wider cloth in place. Knot it at your side leaving a 2-foot (60-cm) fringed "tail." Tuck the fringed end under the wide waistcloth so the fringes hang below.

— KNOT

— FRINGES

ACTIVITY

Boy's Turban

In ancient times, Lachish men and boys made turbans by winding long strips of cloth around and around their heads. You can make a headdress that looks like theirs, but is easier to put on. Have a friend help.

Materials

Old plain bed sheet or piece of cloth at least 5 feet long (150 cm) and 2 feet (60 cm) wide

Tape measure

Scissors

Safety pins (at least 4)

Dinner plate

Pen or pencil

Directions

Cut two strips of cloth at least 5 feet (150 cm) long and about 2½ to 3 inches (6 to 8 cm) wide. The hem of a sheet works well. Pin end-to-end and set aside.

Trace around the dinner plate onto the remaining fabric. Cut out the circle. Cut a straight slit from the edge to the center. Overlap the edges you just cut and pin into a floppy cone shape.

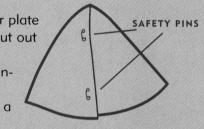

SAFETY PINS

Measure and cut a final piece of fabric into a rectangle about 4 inches by 8 inches (10 x 20 cm). Cut fringes in one end. Pin the other end to the cone's edge.

Put the cone on your head with the fringed end hanging over your right ear. Have your friend wrap the long strip around and around your head, sometimes going over the top of your head, until your hair is hidden. Tuck in the ends securely.

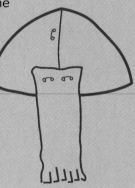

20

ACTIVITY

Girl's Dress

You can dress like a girl from Lachish circa 701 B.C.E. Wear a dress, headscarf (page 22), and sandals or bare feet. You may want to add ankle bracelets (see page 22), earrings, a cylinder seal (see page 28), or other jewelry. Wear a long, unpatterned T-shirt, sleeveless straight dress, or nightgown that hangs to your ankles. The dress should have no ruffles or buttons. Or make a dress with a friend, this way.

Materials

Plain white or colored cloth, twice as long as your body from the your shoulders to your ankles, and as wide as you are from elbow to elbow when your arms are outstretched

Ruler or tape measure

Pencil or pen

Scissors

Safety pins

Directions

Fold the cloth in half the long way. Fold it again, the other way. The cloth should now be as long as your body and half as wide as you are from elbow to elbow. Make sure the edges are even. Find the corner where both folds come together. Be sure you have the correct corner. Pin the layers together nearby. Draw an arc from one side of the corner to the other, 2 to 3 inches (5 to 8 cm) from the corner itself. Cut along the curve, remove the pins, and unfold. You should have a hole big enough for your head. If it's too small, make it *slightly* wider. Put the dress on. Have a friend pin the dress under your arms, one pin per side, not too tight.

SAFETY PINS

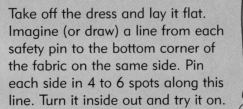

SAFETY PINS

Take off the dress and lay it flat. Imagine (or draw) a line from each safety pin to the bottom corner of the fabric on the same side. Pin each side in 4 to 6 spots along this line. Turn it inside out and try it on.

ACTIVITY

Girl's Headscarf

Materials

Plain-colored piece of cloth as long as you are tall and about 3 feet (1 m) wide

Bobby pins

Directions

Fold back one of the 3-foot-wide (1-m) ends of the cloth a few inches (5 to 7 cm).

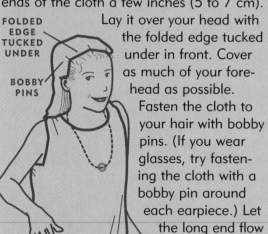

Lay it over your head with the folded edge tucked under in front. Cover as much of your forehead as possible. Fasten the cloth to your hair with bobby pins. (If you wear glasses, try fastening the cloth with a bobby pin around each earpiece.) Let the long end flow over your back and shoulders.

FOLDED EDGE TUCKED UNDER

BOBBY PINS

Armbands or Ankle Bracelets

Many Israelite girls and women wore a pair of plain metal bands, often made of bronze, around their ankles. Men might wear them around their arms. In this activity you can make a pair.

Materials

Masking tape

10 yellow or gold pipe cleaners, each at least 12 inches (30 cm) long

Yellow or gold marker (same color as the pipe cleaners)

Directions

Color about 6 inches (15 cm) of the masking tape while it is still on the roll. Lay 5 pipe cleaners side by side, their ends even. Cover each end with an inch (2.5 cm) of colored tape pressed down firmly. Make a small knob on each end by folding over the tape-covered tips. Place the joined pipe cleaners around your ankle, wrist, or arm. Twist the two knobs together to keep your bracelet on. Make a second bracelet with the remaining pipe cleaners. If the pipe cleaners start to pull apart, take off the bracelet and make a single twist in the middle.

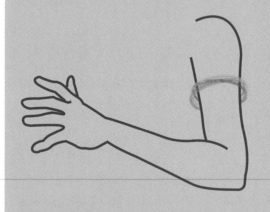

Israelite Language and Writing

The Israelites spoke an ancient form of Hebrew. During the later Iron Age, people spoke it a little differently in the south (Judah) than in the north (Israel), but everyone could understand one another, just as a person from London can understand a New Yorker (most of the time, anyway!).

After exile to Babylonia, the Israelites learned to speak another language: Aramaic (air-a-MAY-ick). This was the language of the Aramaeans (air-a-MAY-ans), a tribal people who lived in Syria, Assyria, and Babylonia during the Iron Age.

Ancient Hebrew and Aramaic were related. Both were members of a language family called Semitic (se-MIH-tick), along with Phoenician and other Canaanite tongues. Modern Semitic languages include Hebrew and Arabic. Compare the word for "peace" in Hebrew—*shalom* (sha-LOME)—with the same word in Arabic—*salaam* (sa-LAHM). Notice how alike they are, and how different they both are from the English word "peace"? That's because modern Hebrew and Arabic are related, just as the ancient Semitic languages were. English, on the other hand, belongs to another language family entirely, called Indo-European.

Ancient Israelite Letter	Ancient Sound	Possible Ancient Letter Name	Modern Hebrew Form
✝	sound made in the throat	Aleph	א
𐤁	B	Bet	ב
𐤂	G	Gimel	ג
𐤃	D	Dalet	ד
𐤄	H	Hay	ה
𐤅	W	Waw	ו
𐤆	Z	Zayin	ז
𐤇	Kh (like clearing the throat)	Khet	ח
⊕	T	Tet	ט
𐤉	Y	Yod	י
𐤊	K	Kaph	כ

Ancient Israelite Letter	Ancient Sound	Possible Ancient Letter Name	Modern Hebrew Form
𐤋	L	Lamed	ל
𐤌	M	Mem	מ
𐤍	N	Nun	נ
𐤎	S	Samek	ס
𐤏	sound made deep in the throat	'Ayin	ע
𐤐	P or F	Pay	פ
𐤑	Ts	Tsadi	צ
𐤒	like K only pronounced deeper in the throat	Qoph (pronounced like Kof)	ק
𐤓	R	Resh	ר
𐤔	Sh or S	Shin or Sin	ש
𐤕	T	Taw	ת

This ancient Israelite alphabet is adapted from one used during Hezekiah's reign (727–698 B.C.E.). Two letters (tet and samek) come from other inscriptions. If you know modern Hebrew, you might see some surprises. For example, in modern Hebrew, aleph is silent, and the letter waw is called vav and pronounced like "V."

D Y Nd Vwls T Rd Nd Wrt?

If you could read the title above, the answer is obviously no! If you couldn't, try this: Th blck ct rn dwn th strt. Did you read *The black cat ran down the street?* (Instead, you might have read *The block cot*—or *cut* or *act*—*run dawn the start*, but that wouldn't make too much sense.) What's missing in that sentence is the vowels. Now try reading the heading again. Could you do it?

The ancient Israelite alphabet had no vowels. People had to guess what vowel sounds went with the consonants, just as you had to do in the sentence about the "blck ct." In modern Israel, vowels are rarely written, except for children or foreigners.

The Ancient Hebrew Alphabet

Around 900 B.C.E., the Israelites—like the Aramaeans and others in the region—were using the 22-letter Phoenician alphabet. (You can read more about the Phoenician alphabet and its history on pages 69 to 71.) As time went on, the Israelites began tweaking the letters' shapes. The Aramaeans and others did the same. With every change, each group's alphabet became more and more individual. By 703 B.C.E., the Israelite alphabet looked like the one on page 24.

But then something happened that would change the future of Hebrew writing forever: the Babylonian Exile. In Babylonia, the Israelites learned a form of the Aramaic alphabet, and began to use it instead of their own. Over time, they even began using it to write their sacred Hebrew books. The modern Hebrew alphabet is based on the Aramaic alphabet, not on the ancient Israelite alphabet. That's why the two alphabets on page 24 look so different.

Today, few people besides scholars use the ancient Israelite alphabet. That makes it very handy for secret messages!

ACTIVITY

Writing Ancient Israelite Style

Try writing your name in the ancient Israelite alphabet. Leave out the vowels.
You can use a yad for "J," and a dalet, tet, or tav for "TH" (or perhaps tet-hay).
Think more about how your name sounds than how you spell it in English.
For example, if your name is Cindy, start it with a letter standing for an "S" sound.
Like the ancient Israelites, write from right to left.

ACTIVITY

Writing on a Smashed Pot

Can you imagine having to do most of your writing on broken clay? Make your own Israelite-style "stationery" by smashing an empty flowerpot (with permission, of course). Your parents may want you to do this outside.

Materials

Clean, unpainted, unglazed, clay flowerpot—3 to 6 inches (7.5 to 15 cm) diameter

Newspaper

Hammer

Broom and dustpan

1 stick of artist's charcoal (available in art stores)

Directions

Place the flowerpot on several sheets of newspaper and fold the sheets over it. Strike the flowerpot with one firm, controlled blow of the hammer.

Pick out the larger pieces to write on and discard the rest. Use the broom to sweep up any that escaped.

Practice writing on the potsherd with charcoal. Write your name and your father's name the way the ancient Israelites did: "Tom son of Michael," or "Tracy daughter of Ben."

On another potsherd, try writing your name and parent's name using the ancient Israelite alphabet on page 24.

If you like, add a secret message for a friend. Hint: If you run out of space on a line in the middle of a word, do what the ancient Israelites did: just finish the word on the next line!

Reading Backward and Other Differences

If you were an ancient Israelite, you might say that people read and write backward in English. That's because we read and write English from left to right. Ancient Israelites read and wrote from right to left—as do modern Arabs and Israelis.

The ancient (and modern) Israelite alphabets have other differences from the alphabet we use for English. Look at the chart on page 24. Did you find any extra letters? There are no letters in English that stand for the same things as aleph, 'ayin, or khet, since those sounds don't appear in English. Likewise, the Israelite alphabet lacks a letter for the sound "J"—since the Israelites didn't use it. What other differences can you find?

Writing Materials

In a world without paper, what would you write on? If the Israelites could afford to, they used parchment (tanned animal skins) or papyrus (mashed stems of the papyrus plant, pressed into a material like paper and imported from Egypt). But parchment and papyrus were expensive. Instead, the Israelites often used broken pottery, called potsherds. A potsherd with writing on it is called an ostracon (OSS-tra-con).

Israelites probably wrote with pencil-sized pieces of wood, with the tips spread apart into a kind of brush. Or they might have used pens made from reed plants. Soot from the bottom of cooking pots, sometimes mixed with iron, water, and a sticky substance from plants, formed their ink.

Seals

Seals are small hard objects carved with their owner's names and perhaps a picture—backward. Often made of bone, stone, ivory, or even gems, a seal let the owner put a "signature" on something made of clay. Here's one example: the owner would stamp the seal onto the handle of a not-quite-dry clay jar. Because the name on the seal was written backward, it would come out forward on the jar. Clay jars from King Hezekiah's time have stamps saying "to the king" in Hebrew.

People could use seals to keep letters private, too—at least letters written on papyrus. They'd roll the letter into a tube, tie it with strings, and put wet blobs of clay over the knots. Then they'd press their seal into the clay. The reader would have to break the clay blobs to untie the cords.

People often wore seals as jewelry, either attached to finger rings or pierced and worn around their necks.

ACTIVITY

Stamp Seal

With this handy object, you can seal a letter like an Israelite. This is much more fun than using an envelope. Adult supervision recommended when baking the clay.

Materials

Oven

Bakeable clay, such as Sculpey, ¼ block per seal

Wooden or metal skewer, long enough to balance across a bowl

Sheet of tracing paper

Pen or pencil

Toothpick or clay tool

Medium to large oven-proof bowl

Potholders

Writing paper

6-inch (15-cm) length of string

Potter's clay or self-drying clay, such as Marblex, about ¼ cup (60 ml)

Directions

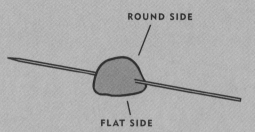

Preheat the oven to the temperature listed on the package of clay.

Shape the clay into a small mound. Round one side and make the other flat and smooth.

Pierce the clay from one end to the other with the skewer. Twist the skewer a few times so the hole gets bigger. Leave the skewer poking through the clay.

Write your name on the tracing paper with pen or pencil. For extra fun, use the ancient Israelite alphabet.

Turn the paper over so your name appears backward.

Scratch your name backward onto the clay's flat side with the toothpick or clay tool. Dig out the letters large and deep, but don't dig as deep as the skewer.

If you like, inscribe a picture on the seal, perhaps an animal.

Lay the skewer across the top of the bowl so that the seal is suspended in the middle of it. Place the bowl in the oven. Bake the clay according to the directions on the package. Wash your hands thoroughly after using bakeable clay.

When the clay is done baking, remove the bowl from the oven with the potholders. Let the seal cool completely before using it or it may break.

While the seal is cooling, write a message (using the English or ancient Israelite alphabet) on a piece of paper.

Roll your message into a tube and tie the string around it.
Shape one tablespoon of the potter's clay into a roundish blob.
Press it on top of the knot.

When your seal is cool, remove it from the skewer.
Press it onto the clay blob, then lift it back off.

Clean your seal with a toothpick after using it, while the clay is still moist.

Wait several days until the clay blob dries. Deliver your message and watch while the person breaks the seal!

The seal on the left belonged to Ya'azanyahu, a royal official who lived sometime between 750 and 650 B.C.E. On the right is what you see when the seal is pressed into clay. Courtesy of the Israel Antiquities Authority.

Israelite Work

Except in a big city like Jerusalem, most ancient Israelites worked as farmers who raised goats and sheep, grew wheat and barley, olives, grapes, and more. Hard work was expected of everyone. Both women and men probably worked at least 10 hours a day in the house or field. By age 13, most children worked nearly as hard. Seven- or eight-year-olds might have worked four hours a day, and even younger children helped gather animal dung for fuel or pulled weeds. Most Israelite farms were small, no bigger than the family could handle, with perhaps a couple of servants to help.

Farming was challenging partly because of the climate. Plants and animals had to withstand long summers without rain, followed by torrential autumn downpours. Droughts, locusts and other pests, disease, and sometimes war added to the difficulties. One way the Israelites dealt with these problems was to raise more than one kind of food. That way, if a storm or disease damaged one kind of crop, the farm family could rely on the others.

Terrace Farming

The early Israelite farmers faced still another challenge: settling on hillsides too steep to grow crops. They solved this problem with terrace farming.

This diagram shows a side view of a terraced hillside. Stone walls hold each level in place. Courtesy of Dr. Shimon Gibson, JAFU, Jerusalem.

Terrace farming meant turning a hillside into something like a staircase for giants. To make each terrace (or giant stairstep) the Israelites first built a long, stone wall around the hillside, then heaped rubble behind the wall until the ground there was flat. Finally, they covered the rubble with soil. They repeated this until long, narrow fields covered the entire side of the hill. On them the Israelites planted wheat and barley; fig, almond, olive, and bushy pomegranate trees; grapevines, beans, and lentils. Sometimes they put different crops on a single terrace— for example, olive trees standing in a field of wheat. Paths let the Israelites climb up and down.

ACTIVITY

Model Terrace Farm

With a dishpan of dirt, you can turn a "hill" into terraces.

Materials

Two pieces of cardboard, one 10 by 8 inches (25 x 20 cm), the other 10 by 6 inches (25 x 15 cm); the backing from notepads works well

Plastic dishpan, 10 by 12 inches (25 x 30 cm)

Masking tape

Dirt, enough to fill ¾ of the plastic dishpan

Directions

Stand the pieces of cardboard upright in the dishpan to make sure they fit without bending.

Trim ends with scissors if necessary.

Fold the cardboard pieces in half the long way so that one is 4 inches wide by 10 inches long (10 x 25 cm), and the other is 3 inches wide by 10 inches long (7.5 x 25 cm). Tape both pieces closed.

TRIM IF NEEDED

Place them parallel to the narrow sides of the dishpan, between the dishpan's two long sides.

Pour the dirt into the dishpan. Shape the dirt into a slope, with the higher side at one narrow end of the dishpan.

Use the cardboard pieces to turn the slope into "terraces." Push them upright into the dirt until they touch the bottom, with the taller one closer to the higher side of the dirt. They should jut an inch or so above the slope. Shape the dirt into a "step" behind each piece of cardboard.

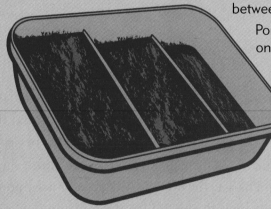

Children are riding a donkey past terraced hills near modern Jerusalem.
Courtesy of Garo Nalbandian.

ACTIVITY

A Balancing Act: Carrying Water

Materials

Tupperware or other plastic
container full of water

Lid

Clothes you don't mind getting wet

Directions

Stand very straight. Balance the covered
container of water on your head. (You
might need help to do this.) Walk a few
steps.

Now imagine doing this for two miles
with a heavy, breakable clay jar on your
head!

Terraces helped the Israelites grow crops despite the climate. Without terraces, water from heavy rains would rush downhill so fast that it barely sank into the earth to water crops. The rain could also wash away soil. Terraces helped conserve the precious water. Rain falling on each terrace either stayed there, or trickled through the wall to the terrace below—not too much and not too little. Because they were built without mortar, the walls had many small holes for water to drip through.

Building terraces and repairing the walls were huge tasks. Usually an entire village would organize the project.

Men's Work and Women's Work

On farms, men and women worked equally hard but probably did different things. Most plowing, planting, and mending of terrace walls were probably done by men and boys. These jobs took strength as well as skill. Because they often tended small children, women and girls probably stayed closer to the house, doing things they could interrupt more easily: grinding grain, preparing cheese and yogurt, cooking, making baskets, shaping clay pots, spinning thread, weaving fabric, sewing clothing, and so on. Women needed many different skills to perform all these tasks well—plus strength and patience. (Imagine pushing a grindstone for hours a day—it would build muscles fast!)

Women and girls also hauled water home from wells or springs, often tramping two miles (3.2 km) each way carrying heavy clay jars on their heads. Although terribly hard, the job had one good side—it gave them a chance to chat with others at the wells. They may have had few other chances to talk with people outside their families. Some jobs were done by everyone in the family. Harvesting crops probably took everyone's help. Either boys or girls might be shepherds. Some tasks—like stomping grapes into juice—might have been done by the whole community, with music and dancing.

A woman carried an empty clay water jar upside-down on her head in this photo taken in Palestine 75 years ago. Courtesy of the Palestine Exploration Fund.

City Work

City and townspeople who worked as farmers left each day to tend fields beyond the city walls. Men could also be soldiers, government officials, craftsmen, or merchants, while women managed households, wove, made clothing, and prepared food, much as they did on farms. Male or female city-dwellers might also be servants or slaves for others. City women could be cooks, bakers, or perfume-makers for the king.

Working in Exile

During their exile in Babylonia, the people from Judah lived in a fertile area near a river, probably farming the land and fishing. Ancient records show that Israelites worked as craftsmen on Nebuchadnezzar's building projects. Over time, some grew wealthy. Some Israelites came to feel at home in Babylonia. Not everyone chose to return to Judah when they could.

Israelite Food

Today, if we're hungry, what do we do? We pop something in the microwave, slap a slice of cheese between two pieces of bread, or open a can of soup. Preparing a meal, at least a simple one, can take less than five minutes. Imagine how an Israelite might feel if he or she could watch us make lunch. For most Israelites, every meal meant hours of work: growing crops, grinding grain, pressing olive oil, milking goats, and so on.

The Pleasures of Meat

Bread was the Israelites' most important food, but their favorite was probably meat. Since eating meat meant killing a sheep, goat, or calf, they usually served it only on holidays, or for important guests. Israelites also ate some fish, and fowl, such as pigeons and geese. Chickens probably didn't exist in Israel until about 800 B.C.E.

Not all meat was considered suitable. For example, the Bible forbids eating pork. Archaeologists have found very few pig bones in Israelite ruins from this period.

The Israelites also liked fruit: pomegranates, figs, dates, raisins, and grapes. They ate vegetables, too: beans, peas, chickpeas, lentils, wild onions, lettuce, and cucumber. Goats and sheep, as well as cows, gave them milk, used for butter, white cheese, and perhaps yogurt. Besides milk, the Israelites drank water, wine, and probably grape juice. Other foods included

This ibex (a type of wild goat) lives in a modern Israeli nature preserve. Ancient Israelite hunters sometimes shot ibex, deer, and antelope for food.
Photo by Dan and Sis Polin.

In this photo taken about 75 years ago, a woman from Palestine carried an enormous bundle of twigs. Gathering fuel was a never-ending job.
Courtesy of the Palestine Exploration Fund.

almonds, wild birds' eggs, and grain toasted over a fire or mixed into porridge. The rich ate a more varied diet than the poor.

For flavoring, the Israelites used olive oil and salt, and probably herbs and spices such as cumin, coriander, dill, sage, mint, and thyme. In the Bible, Ruth dipped her bread in vinegar. Israelites probably also spread bread with honey, date jam, or grape juice boiled down into syrup.

Ancient Israelites wouldn't have recognized a potato, tomato, peanut, orange, lemon, or green pepper. All these foods came into the region much later. It's sad to think the Israelites never tasted chocolate.

Grapes and Olives

The olive tree and the grapevine gave the Israelites many different foods. See how many foods you can find that come from these plants. Easy to miss is vinegar, which the Israelites made from wine.

To make wine, the Israelites stomped on grapes in special stone vats. Then they collected the juice in large clay jars, with small holes at the top to let gases escape. When the wine was ready they sealed the jars completely.

Making Bread Like an Israelite

Here's how an Israelite girl might make bread.

First, she'd spend hours on her knees, pushing a heavy stone across wheat or barley grains to make flour—hard work and boring! With luck, her house would have two sets of grindstones, so her sister or mother could grind beside her and chat.

She'd mix the flour with water, yeast, and perhaps oil and salt.

She'd knead and shape the dough into loaves, and perhaps let them rise.

Early in the morning, she'd start a fire in a fire pit or oven. She might get her little brother or sister to gather animal dung or branches for fuel. For kindling, she'd use twigs, or the mashed olives and olive pits left from making oil.

She'd set the loaves to bake on clay trays pierced with holes. Or she might slap circles of dough directly onto the oven's inner walls. They'd stick there and bake.

She'd serve and—finally—eat the bread. She'd probably have help for *this* step!

She'd repeat all this work every day of the week except the Sabbath—the one day set aside for prayer and rest.

Ancient Israelite "Table" Manners

Unless they were rich enough to own a table, most Israelites probably ate on the floor while squatting around platters. Before eating, they may have washed their hands and said a blessing. Then, using their fingers, family members would put food from the platter into their own bowls, or straight into their mouths. If the food was soup or stew, they might ladle it into their bowls and drink it, or use a bit of bread as a spoon.

Most people probably drank wine mixed with water at meals. They dipped a small jug into a pottery jar filled with wine, poured it into each person's drinking bowl (called a "kos"), then added water. Today, "kos" is the Hebrew word for drinking glass.

Still unripe, these figs grow on a tree near the city of Dan. Fruit such as pomegranates, figs, and grapes added sweetness to the ancient Israelites' lives. Courtesy of Scott Noegel.

ACTIVITY

Stomping Grapes into Juice

You can make grape juice the way ancient Israelites did—with your feet.
Don't try this if you have cuts on your feet—it stings! Adult supervision recommended for mess control.

Materials

- 3 pounds (1.4 kg) fresh red or purple grapes, seedless is best
- Clean dishpan or large, deep pot
- Self-stick label and pen
- Jar with lid
- 2 large plastic garbage bags
- VERY clean feet
- Damp washcloth and towels
- Large wire sieve (mesh fine enough to catch grape seeds) or colander lined with 4 layers of cheesecloth
- Bowl large enough to hold the sieve or colander
- Funnel
- Small bowls for drinking

Directions

Wash your hands and the grapes. Throw away the grape stems and moldy or overripe grapes. Place the other grapes in a dishpan. Label the jar with your name as the juicemaker, perhaps using the ancient Israelite alphabet (on page 24.) Spread the garbage bags onto the ground. Place the grape-filled dishpan on the bags.

Now for the fun part: With clean feet, step into the dishpan and smoosh the grapes with your feet.

Wipe your feet with the damp washcloth before stepping out. Discard the plastic garbage bags.

Place the sieve or colander inside the pot or bowl. Carefully pour the juice through the sieve or colander to strain out the seeds, pulp, and skin. Use clean hands to squoosh out the extra juice. Place the funnel in the jar. Pour the strained juice into the funnel.

Drink the juice from small bowls, or refrigerate to drink later with an ancient Israelite meal. Use within a few days.

Yum! Did you taste any toe jam?

ACTIVITY

Ancient Israelite Meal

You can serve and eat a meal ancient Israelite-style. The most important part? Eating with your hands.

Materials

Fresh or dried fruit such as pomegranates, raisins, dates, grapes, or figs

Pita bread

Bite-sized pieces of feta or other white cheese

Sliced cucumbers, green onions, or torn lettuce leaves

Large platter, tray, or wide-mouthed bowl

Small cup, jar, or ladle for dipping up juice

Large pot, bowl, or wide-mouth jar containing grape juice

Small bowls for drinking

Napkins

Pitcher of cool water

Medium-sized bowls for eating

Saucer with honey or vinegar

Directions

Wash your hands and arrange the food on a platter, tray, or large bowl. Use the cup, jar, or ladle to dip up juice and pour it into drinking bowls. Use the napkins to clean up any juice that may have dripped. Add water from the pitcher to each drinking bowl. Set the food on the floor along with bowls for eating and drinking. Have people sit or squat around the food and serve themselves with clean fingers. If you like, before eating, say a blessing over the food and juice.

Eat with your hands. Try dipping bread into honey or vinegar before eating it. To end the meal, clean your empty bowl with bread, then eat the bread.

Israelite Religion

According to the biblical book of Exodus (EX-o-duss), God gave the Ten Commandments to Moses on top of Mount Sinai. As lightning flashed and smoke wreathed the mountain, God uttered the second commandment: "You shall have no other gods beside me."

Today, Jews, Christians, Muslims, and others share the concept of a single God. But during ancient Israelite times, this idea was rare indeed. Many scholars think that at first, the Israelites believed that other gods existed—even if they themselves were to worship only God. It may have taken centuries for the Israelites to come to believe that God was the only true power in the universe.

The Canaanites believed in and worshipped many deities, including the gods El and Baal (BA-al), and the goddesses Astarte (as-TAR-tay), Anath (a-NATH), and Asherah (a-shay-RA). Like nearly everyone in the region, they prayed to each god for a different reason: some gods to protect their city and family, and other gods for healing, help with their work, or a good harvest. They believed that each god or goddess had separate responsibilities, and all needed to be worshipped for the world to be whole and safe.

Remember the Sabbath Day

The fourth commandment is to "remember the Sabbath day and keep it holy." The word "Sabbath" comes from the Hebrew word "Shabbat," meaning to stop, as in stopping work. The Bible instructs the Israelites to do no work on the seventh day of each week, from sunset to sunset. (To the ancient Israelites, each day began and ended at sunset—a system modern Jews still follow for religious holidays.)

Priests and Sacrifices

According to the Bible, all the men from the tribe of Levi, the Levites, had religious jobs. Most were priests' helpers, while a few were priests. (During the United Monarchy, non-Levites were priests too.) Priests interpreted religious law, settled disputes, blessed the Israelites and cursed lawbreakers, and sometimes blew a ram's horn. Their most important job, however, was offering sacrifices.

Priests made sacrifices to God on behalf of the Israelite people or specific individuals. Most often, they offered cattle, goats, sheep, birds, baked goods, incense, or wine. Most

This altar once stood in the ancient city of Megiddo. Too small to hold an animal, it was probably used for burning incense. Courtesy of the Oriental Institute of the University of Chicago.

43

Imagining a Day Without Work

Imagine living in ancient Israel, without running water, refrigeration, electricity, matches, or ice. You work terribly hard six days a week.

Now imagine that each week, from one sundown to the next, you are not allowed to work. Nor may you light a new fire, cook, gather food or fuel or ask others (including non-Israelites) to do these things for you.

Not working sounds nice, doesn't it? But can you imagine any problems? For example: What food can you prepare in advance that wouldn't spoil in the summer heat? What if you're sick and need extra heat and food, and your fire goes out? Should you milk animals on the Sabbath? (If you don't milk them, they suffer pain.)

Keeping the Sabbath meant planning for all these possibilities. People were allowed to care for babies, serve meals, and milk animals. Still, the Sabbath was mostly a time for rest. As much as possible, things were done in advance or put off for another day.

sacrifices were burned on altars. Four raised corners on the altar, called "horns," may have helped keep the offering on top.

Sacrifices involved rituals. In one, the priest dabbed blood on the right ear, right thumb, and right big toe of the person bringing the animal for sacrifice.

Women Religious Leaders

Only men worked as priests or Levites, but women as well as men could be prophets. Many Israelites believed that prophets were holy people who could voice God's wishes and predict events in the future. Many prophets spoke out on behalf of the poor and downtrodden.

Women prophets in the Bible included Deborah, Huldah, and Moses' sister Miriam. Huldah was so important that King Josiah (jo-ZIE-ah) turned to her for advice when, around 622 B.C.E., workmen in the Temple found a mysterious scroll of religious law. According to the Bible, Huldah—inspired by the scroll—foretold disaster for the people of Judah, but said that Josiah would die before it struck. Her prediction came true. Some years after Josiah's death, Nebuchadnezzar attacked and eventually destroyed Jerusalem.

Other Gods and Goddesses

The Bible clearly states that the Israelites were to worship only one God. But it also tells stories of Israelites worshipping Baal, Astarte, Asherah, and others. It describes Israelites worshipping these gods in "high places" such as hilltops, sometimes erecting a tree or pole called an asherah, like the goddess. It even mentions some Israelites sacrificing children to other gods.

The Name of God

We don't know for sure what the Israelites called their God in prayer. In writing, they used four letters: *yod hay waw hay*. Today, many scholars treat these letters as a name: Yahweh (yah-WEH). A few centuries ago, Bible translators incorrectly pronounced the same letters "Jehovah" (je-HOE-vah).

When modern Jews read these Hebrew letters in a prayer book, they don't try to pronounce them. Instead, they say a Hebrew word that means "my Lord." (In modern Hebrew, the letter "waw" has become "vav.")

Archaeologists may have found evidence for some of this worship. On a hilltop near several early Israelite settlements they found the bronze figure of a bull. Nearby was a large stone, possibly an altar. Some archaeologists believe Israelites may have worshipped the Canaanite god El on that spot, since El's symbol was a bull.

Archaeologists have also found a few inscriptions in the Sinai desert and Judah mentioning "YHWH and his Asherah." How should they interpret these? Did some Israelites use a tree or pole to worship God? Or—as some scholars maintain—did some Israelites believe that Asherah was God's wife?

Where to Worship?

During the period of Judges, the Bible tells us that the Israelites had outdoor places of worship—for example, at a town called Shiloh. Some people may also have had altars for their own families' use.

When King Solomon built the Temple in Jerusalem, it became the most important center of worship in the land. Priests made sacrifices there at least twice daily. During their reigns, Kings Hezekiah and Josiah smashed and burned many of the outdoor centers of worship, trying to make the Temple in Jerusalem the center for all worship. They believed that the smaller centers encouraged the worship of other gods.

Not everyone was happy about centering worship in Jerusalem. Around 925 B.C.E., King Jeroboam I re-established religious centers in two cities—northern Dan and Bethel, near Jerusalem. Archaeologists have found signs of an enormous "high place" and altars in Dan.

When Nebuchadnezzar of Babylon conquered Judah in 587 B.C.E., he destroyed the Temple in Jerusalem and exiled many of the Israelites to Babylonia. Without their Temple, they no longer sacrificed animals and had to develop new rituals that focused on prayer, the Sabbath, and holy texts. They brought these changes back to Jerusalem when they were allowed to go home.

ACTIVITY

Blessing Scroll

You can make a blessing scroll like the ones found in ancient Israel.

Materials

Heavy-duty aluminum foil, about 4 inches by 1½ inches (10 x 4 cm)

Ballpoint pen

Embroidery floss or thin string at least 2 feet (60 cm) long

Transparent tape

Directions

Pressing firmly with the pen, write a blessing on one side of the foil—for example, "May you have peace."

Make sure the floss is long enough to go over your head easily, with a few extra inches for a knot.

Lay the middle of the floss along one short end of the foil.

Starting at one end, roll the foil into a neat tube.

Tape it closed. Knot the ends together. Make sure the floss is long enough to go over your head easily.

Wear your blessing scroll, or give it to someone you care about.

A Familiar Prayer

From an ancient cemetery in a Jerusalem valley, archaeologists dug up two tiny scrolls of crumbling silver, dated near the time of the Babylonian exile. On these bits of silver, some ancient silversmith had engraved Hebrew verses, then rolled them into tubes. Translated, the verses read: "May God bless you and keep you. May God cause his face to shine upon you and give you peace."

Thousands of years later, people around the world still recognize these words. They appear, in a slightly longer form, in the Bible. Many Jewish parents use them to bless their children each Sabbath, while some Christians use them as a prayer during baptism or at the close of church services.

Conclusion

The ancient Israelites left us a number of legacies, with the most important one being the Hebrew Bible. Sacred to both Jews and Christians, this book has influenced cultures on every continent.

Another Israelite legacy is the Sabbath. Today, observant Muslims, Christians, and Jews all set aside one day a week for rest and special religious observance. The actual day is different—Friday for Muslims, Saturday for Jews, and Sunday for most Christians—but the idea is very much the same.

If you want an everyday example of the Israelites' influence, think about names. Do you know anyone named David, Deborah, Jonathan, Sarah, Rebecca, Joseph, or Rachel? Taken from the Hebrew Bible, these names—and many others—once belonged to ancient Israelites. People speaking other languages use biblical names, too. For example, Michel (mee-SHEL) and Miguel (mee-GALE), are forms of the Israelite name Mee-kha-EL (Michael in English).

Some last names, such as Cohen, also preserve the Israelite heritage. Ancestors of people named Cohen (ko-HANE in Hebrew, the word for priest) probably carried out priestly duties in Israelite times.

Would the ancient Israelites be surprised that parts of their heritage live on? It's hard to say. Surely our world today is amazingly different from theirs. Cell phones, televisions, freeways, computers, airplanes and—unfortunately—bombs and guns might overshadow the similarities that remain. What do you think King Solomon would say if he could see the land he once ruled today?

PART 2

THE PHOENICIANS

Israel, Phoenicia, and Philistia during the Iron Age.

49

Phoenician History

Bold seafarers, famous navigators, talented traders, skilled craftspeople, the Phoenicians brought objects of luxury and beauty to people in near and distant lands. Their home base was a string of city-states along the coast in Lebanon (LEB-a-non), the name of northern coastal Canaan in both ancient and modern times.

From these city-states, the Phoenicians established a vast trading empire, linking lands in Europe, Asia, and northern Africa. Sturdy Phoenician ships carried richly dyed cloth, metal ingots, wine, and other goods from city to city and coast to coast around the entire Mediterranean Sea.

The name "Phoenician" comes to us from the Greek word "phoinix" (POY-nik-es) meaning purple or dark red. The word referred to the Phoenicians' most famous product, purple dye, made from small sea creatures like snails.

Geography

The Phoenicians' homeland was a narrow strip of seacoast squeezed between the tree-covered Lebanon Mountains and the Mediterranean Sea. Their most famous city, Tyre, stood on a series of islands just off shore. The cities Byblos, Sidon, Sarepta, and Berytus (bare-EE-tus)—which became the modern city of Beirut (bay-ROOT)—arose beside natural harbors along the coast, while the city Arwad (ar-WAD), like Tyre, stood on an island.

This drawing of a wall carving shows Assyrian soldiers plundering a Phoenician city, possibly Tyre.
From A. H. Layard, *A Second Series of the Monuments of Nineveh*, Pl. 40. Courtesy of the University of Pennsylvania Museum (Neg. #NC35-22007).

The Story of Wen-Amun

An Egyptian tale, written down about 1100 B.C.E., shows the value of Phoenician cedars and tells us something about relations between the Phoenicians and their neighbors during the early Iron Age.

In the story, an Egyptian named Wen-Amun (wen-a-MOON) sailed to Byblos to buy cedar for rebuilding the boat of an Egyptian god. On the way, he stopped at Dor, capital of a sea people called the Sikils. There, one of his sailors ran off with most of his silver and gold. Wen-Amun demanded that the Sikil ruler, named Beder, replace what was stolen, but Beder refused. Instead the ruler offered to search for the thief, but the thief wasn't found.

Frustrated, Wen-Amun set sail again for Byblos. On the way, he "borrowed" some silver from a Sikil ship, saying he would return it when his own silver was found.

When Wen-Amun finally arrived in Byblos, the city's ruler—the stern Zakar-Baal (za-KAR-ba-AL)—ordered him to leave. Week after week Wen-Amun sought a ship to take him home, but found none headed for Egypt. Finally Zakar-Baal agreed to give Wen-Amun a small amount of timber, but not enough to build the sacred boat. Wen-Amun sent a message by ship to Egypt's rulers, pleading for more goods to trade. In time a ship arrived in Byblos loaded with goods for Zakar-Baal: gold and silver jars, 10 pieces of linen cloth, 10 fine linen garments, 500 blank scrolls of papyrus, 500 ox hides, 500 ropes, 20 bags of lentils and—last but not least—30 baskets of dried fish. Only when these arrived did Zakar-Baal part with more logs.

When Wen-Amun was ready to leave, he discovered 11 Sikil ships lying in wait for him in the harbor! Perhaps they wanted the silver that Wen-Amun had taken from them earlier. Somehow, he managed to sail right past them. But his adventures still weren't over. His ship was blown to the island of Cyprus (SIGH-pruss) where the people threatened him with death. Sadly, the end of the story is lost.

From hillsides thick with cedar, cypress, fir, and pine trees, the Phoenicians cut timber for their own use and for trade. The Hebrew Bible reports that Solomon paneled the walls of the Temple in Jerusalem with fragrant cedar from Lebanon. Rulers throughout the ancient Near East, including Egypt, sought Lebanese logs for building ships, temples, and palaces.

Phoenicians and Culture

The Phoenicians carried on much of earlier Canaanite culture. Why? Because they really *were* Canaanites. (Scholars call them Canaanites during the Bronze Age and Phoenicians in the Iron Age.) As traders, they came to know many other cultures as well. They used symbols from these cultures in their own arts and crafts, which they traded from city to city. Thus an Assyrian nobleman might own a Phoenician silver bowl with Syrian designs, and an Israelite princess might treasure a Phoenician ivory comb with Egyptian symbols.

The Phoenicians spread something more important than these trade goods. They spread the alphabet, the ancestor of the both the English and Hebrew alphabets.

Rise of the City-States

The Phoenician city-states arose during the Bronze Age at the same time as other Canaanite city-states were developing farther south. Even in those early times, the Phoenicians (or northern Canaanites) were traders. But powerful neighboring peoples controlled much of the trade during the Bronze Age, and limited how much the Phoenicians could do.

Around 1200 B.C.E., misfortune struck many of the peoples surrounding the Phoenicians. Mighty Egypt weakened, the Hittite capital fell, and the Syrian city of Ugarit (OO-ga-rit), itself a famous center of trade, collapsed. But the Phoenician cities remained mostly unharmed. With less competition, the Phoenicians soon began expanding their trade. They undertook voyages to more distant lands and carried a bigger supply of costly luxury goods to eager customers.

The Phoenician city-states were not united. Each had its own king and its own fleet of ships, and competed with one another for trade. At times, Tyre was the most powerful; at other times, Sidon. Byblos, the oldest of Phoenician cities, always remained influential.

The Story of King Hiram

The most famous king in all Phoenicia was Hiram I (HI-ram the first), who ruled Tyre from 969 to 936 B.C.E. Under his rule, Tyre became the greatest of the Phoenician cities.

According to the Bible, Hiram sent skilled workers to build David's palace and Solomon's Temple. In exchange, David sent Hiram food supplies, and Solomon gave him control over a number of cities in northern Israel. Together Hiram and Solomon sent sailors and ships to a mysterious land called Ophir (oh-FEER). The ships returned laden with gold, silver, ivory, sandalwood, precious stones, peacocks, and apes. No one is sure, today, where Ophir really was.

Hiram's descendants ruled Tyre for many generations. His descendant Jezebel (JEZ-e-bel) married Ahab, a king of Israel.

Assaults from Without

Beginning around 1100 B.C.E., fierce Assyrian kings demanded tribute from Phoenician city-states. At first, each time the Phoenicians paid their tribute, the Assyrians left them alone, and the Phoenician king-doms kept growing in wealth and power. But

The Founding of Carthage

Greek and Roman writers tell a story about the founding of Carthage around 814 B.C.E. The star of the story is Elissa (e-LISS-a), sometimes called Dido (DIE-doe), the sister of the king of Tyre. She and her supporters fled Tyre after the king killed her husband, a priest who may have been competing for the throne. Eventually they sailed to the coast of Africa where Elissa and her followers wanted land to build a city. Although she had little money for land, she used cunning to make it stretch. Elissa told the local people that she would buy the amount of land that she could cover by an oxhide. They laughed, thinking she was foolish to want so little land. But Elissa was clever: she cut the oxhide into very thin strips, and laid the strips around a large hill. The inhabitants (so the story goes), impressed by her cunning, let her have the hill. The newcomers named the hill "Byrsa" (BUR-sa), which means "oxhide" in Greek. It became the hill on which the city of Carthage stood.

several centuries later, in the 700s, the Assyrian kings sought to make the Phoenician kingdoms part of their empire. The cities fought back, but the Assyrians won. First Assyria destroyed Sidon, then brought Tyre to its knees. The Phoenicians revolted a number of times, but each time the Assyrians defeated them. Then the Assyrian empire fell to the Babylonians in 612 B.C.E.

Like the Assyrians, the Babylonians sought tribute from the Phoenician cities. Tyre and Sidon revolted, along with Judah and other states. After destroying Jerusalem in 587 B.C.E., the Babylonian king Nebuchadnezzar II attacked Phoenicia. For 13 years, his soldiers surrounded Tyre. Although Tyre survived, the Phoenician cities became poorer and less independent. When the Persians defeated Babylonia in 538 B.C.E., the Phoenicians' fortunes began to improve once more.

Colonies

While Assyria pressured Tyre for tribute, the Phoenicians began building colonies in other lands ringing the Mediterranean Sea—in Spain, on the islands of Malta and Cyprus, and in northern Africa. These colonies helped the Phoenicians maintain their wealth.

Among the Phoenician colonies, the most famous of all was Carthage (KAR-thij), a Phoenician name meaning "New City." Built on the North African coast, Carthage grew more and more powerful until it developed an empire of its own, competing with the Greeks—and later the Romans—for trade. In 550 B.C.E., a general from Carthage defeated the Greeks in Sicily. Far more warlike than the Phoenicians from Lebanon, the people of Carthage hired foreign armies and fought the Greeks and Romans for many long years in the centuries after the period covered by this book.

The Phoenicians—Good or Bad?

The Phoenicians earned envy and respect for their wealth and luxury and their skills in ship-building, craftwork, and trade. But they inspired scorn as well, particularly among their trading rivals. A blind Greek poet named Homer called the Phoenicians "lying cheating scoundrels." Other Greeks reported that the Phoenicians kidnapped boys and traded them as slaves. Even worse, ancient Greeks claimed the Phoenicians sacrificed their own children to the gods. It's not wise to believe the tales of the Phoenicians' enemies without probing further. But some of these stories may have been true.

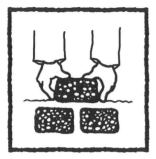

Phoenician Architecture

The Phoenicians built fine cities. So elegant was the ancient Phoenician city of Tyre that the Israelite prophet Ezekiel called it "perfect in beauty." Tyre is now utterly destroyed. But from ancient descriptions, we know it had much in common with other Phoenician cities both in Lebanon and in Phoenician colonies.

The Island City of Tyre

Tyre was a city built on an island. Its name in Phoenician, Sor, means rock. During the Iron Age, the only way to come and go was by boat. Two ports served the city: one to the south and one to the north.

Ringing the city of Tyre stood a tall, stone wall topped with watchtowers where soldiers paced. Massive arched gates allowed people in and out. Tall houses of several stories ranged inside the city wall. On the highest hill within the wall rose the king's palace, its windows looking out over the sea. Nearby stood the grand temples to Tyre's chief goddess and god, Astarte and Melqart (mel-KART). The twin pillars in front of Melqart's temple—rumored to be made of emerald and gold—glittered in the sun.

Across the city from the palace lay the main harbor and the market square. All around the area rose houses of many stories where people fashioned objects of pottery, jewelry, and cloth.

In this Phoenician ivory carving, a woman looks out of a window. Phoenician windows may have had stone railings like this one, with elegant carved columns. Courtesy of Musées royaux d'Art et d'Histoire, Brussels.

This drawing of a wall carving shows Assyrian soldiers plundering a Phoenician city, possibly Tyre.
From A. H. Layard, *A Second Series of the Monuments of Nineveh*, Pl. 40. Courtesy of the University of Pennsylvania Museum (Neg. #NC35-22007).

As far from the palace as possible stood workshops for making purple dye, dried fish, or metal objects. All these industries put out foul stenches. Rich people lived as far from them as they could.

An ancient carving of a Phoenician city—perhaps Tyre—showed tall houses or temples with small high windows and flat roofs. Trees or bushes grew on many rooftops, their tops shaped like domes. Tall columns stood beside the front doors of many buildings. Windows had decorated railings in front. The result was lovely—at least, without some of the smells.

ACTIVITY

Model of Tyre

You can make a model of the city of Tyre, that shows the Phoenician style of architecture. Plan to make it in one day, then allow one week for drying. Adult supervision is recommended.

Materials

1 cup (240 ml) baking soda

½ cup (120 ml) cornstarch

Medium-sized pot

¾ cup (180 ml) warm water

Large spoon

Yellow food coloring

Stove

Potholder

2 heavy paper plates (such as Chinet), or 2 blue plastic plates

Mixing bowl

Newspaper or other table protection

2-foot-long (60-cm) piece of aluminum foil

Fine-tipped black marker

Scissors

8-by-10-inch piece of thin posterboard or cardboard

Optional: wide-tipped blue marker

Directions

Mix the baking soda and cornstarch in the pot. Add the water and stir. Drip in two or three drops of yellow food coloring and stir again. Cook over medium heat, stirring constantly. Use a potholder if the pot handle gets hot. Let the mixture boil, then keep cooking and stirring until it gets as thick as mashed potatoes. Scoop it onto one of the plates to cool. You must use the mixture within 30 minutes, before it hardens.

Spread newspaper on your work surface.

If using a white paper plate, use the blue marker to make it sea-colored.

DOUGH

FOIL

Ball up the aluminum foil and place it on the paper or plastic plate. Cover the foil ball with cooled dough, making an island shape (not too steep). Make sure at least ¼ inch (6 mm) of dough covers all the foil.

Use the picture of the Phoenician city on page 58 as a guide. Draw and cut out posterboard or cardboard pieces of the city wall. Be sure they're the right size for your hill. Make the walls extra long so that there is enough to stick deep into the dough. Use the thin black marker to decorate both sides. Arrange the wall around the hill's edges. Copy and cut out buildings and trees. Draw columns, windows, and rooftop trees like the ones in the picture. Again, decorate both sides. Arrange them in the dough inside the wall. After about two hours, your dough will be too hard to add more buildings.

Use any extra dough to make boats and a dock or two.

Allow about two days for the top of the city to dry. Carefully prop the city on the edge of the plate or tip it on its side to allow the underside to dry too.

TAB TO GO
INTO DOUGH

Phoenician Clothing

The Phoenicians left no clothing from the Iron Age, but a few carvings show us what they wore.

Some men and women wore ankle-length tunics or dresses, sometimes with a fringed hem or—for men—a sash. Sleeves could be long, short, or elbow-length. Men's tunics sometimes stopped just below the knees. Wealthy Phoenicians probably wore clothing dyed bright red, blue, and purple, with fancy weaving and embroidery.

Men wore beards and long or short hair, at times elaborately curled. Women seem to have worn their hair long, with bangs. They may have curled their hair or pinned it up. Fashions and hairstyles probably changed over time, for both women and men.

Women sometimes wore a tall round cap covered by a veil. The veil fell down their backs and alongside their faces. (See the illustration of people in ships on page 74.) Men sometimes wore a soft peaked cap, like an elf's.

We don't know anything about what children wore. Tiny children may have gone naked or worn a cloth draped around their hips. Older children may have dressed like their parents.

The Phoenicians made huge amounts of jewelry to trade, and probably wore a lot themselves—men as well as women. Wealthy people might have worn necklaces, pendants, tiaras, earrings, bracelets, and finger rings of gold or silver. Poorer people might have worn jewelry made of bronze.

Phoenicians sometimes wore flat sandals. They probably also wore boots or went barefoot, depending on the weather and their work.

Seashell Dyeing

Today, broken shells lie in huge piles near ancient Phoenician cities: the remains of small sea creatures related to snails. The Phoenicians used thousands of these creatures to make a single ounce of purple dye—a dye so costly that only the rich could afford it. The Phoenicians' purple dye stayed vivid for a long time, making it highly prized. Other ancient dyes, made from plants, tended to fade quickly with sunlight and washing.

Making the dye was stinky. The Phoenicians gathered the sea snails from shallow waters and left them in pools of salt water to die and rot. After a time they removed the shells and added water to the dye. By using different species of snail and different strengths of dye, they could produce colors from deep red to deep purple to pale pink.

About Mordants

Metals and other chemicals, called mordants, help most colors attach to the fabric and stay bright despite washing. Modern synthetic dyes often contain built-in mordants. A common mordant is a form of aluminum called alum, available in garden or craft stores. Mordants require a few extra safety precautions. For more information about dyes and mordants, consult a book on dyeing.

The Phoenicians used these three kinds of sea creatures to make purple dye. The one on the left made a bluer dye than the others. Courtesy of the American Schools of Oriental Research.

ACTIVITY

Long Dress or Tunic

A Phoenician costume for boys or girls starts with a long- or short-sleeved T-shirt (no pattern or buttons) or a long straight dress with or without sleeves. Girls or boys can follow directions for making the Israelite girl's dress on page 21. Girls' dresses are ankle-length; boys' can be too, or can stop just below the knees.

Materials

- Plain T-shirt (no patterns or buttons) or a long, straight dress
- Scissors
- Wide purple marker or fabric paint
- Sash (boys only)

Directions

With adult permission, cut 2-inch (5-cm) fringes in the bottom hem of the tunic or dress. Above the fringes, color a 2-inch (5-cm) purple stripe around the bottom of the garment. For boys, tie the sash around your waist.

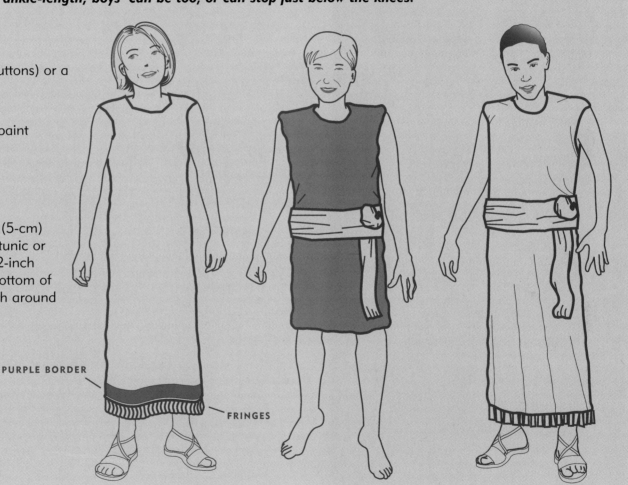

PURPLE BORDER

FRINGES

ACTIVITY

Man's Soft Cap

Adult supervision recommended for sewing.

Materials

Measuring tape

Piece of cloth at least 30 inches by 12 inches (75 x 30 cm)

Pencil

Scissors

Several straight or safety pins

Needle and thread

Optional: waterproof markers or fabric paint

Directions

Measure straight around your head just above the eyebrows. Write down the number, add 5 inches (10 cm), and divide by two. Measure this distance along one edge of the cloth and make a mark. (This measurement will form a base for a large triangle, 12 inches (30 cm) tall. Make sure there will be enough room on the fabric for two triangles this size.)

Mark a dot in the center of the length you measured (the base). Measure 12 inches (30 cm) straight up and make another dot. Draw a line from this dot to one end of your base. Use a ruler or book to help you draw a straight line. Draw a second line from the dot to the other end of the base.

Cut out the triangle. Lay it elsewhere on the cloth and trace around it. Cut out the second triangle. Put one on top of the other and pin them together so the edges match.

Sew along each side of the triangle, but not along the base. Remove pins as you go along.

Turn the hat inside out. If you like, decorate it with markers or fabric paint. Put it on with the seams over your ears. Let the point flop toward the back of your head.

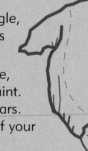

ACTIVITY

Woman's Headdress

Materials

Posterboard 28 inches long and 10 inches wide (70 x 25 cm)

Pencil

Scissors

Ruler

Stapler

Duct tape

Old pillowcase

Safety pin

Directions

Have someone wrap the wide edge of the posterboard around your head just above your ears, snugly. Mark the spot where it overlaps. Remove. Measure 2 inches (5 cm) past the mark and make another mark. Trim off extra posterboard beyond the second mark.

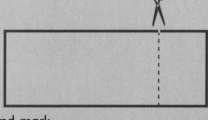

Use a ruler to draw a straight line the length of the posterboard 10 inches (25 cm) up from the bottom. Cut along this line.

Staple the posterboard into a ring the size of your head, with the sharp points of the staples poking out. Test to make sure it fits and is firmly stapled.

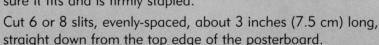

Cut 6 or 8 slits, evenly-spaced, about 3 inches (7.5 cm) long, straight down from the top edge of the posterboard.

Fold these sections in toward the center. Tape together with several pieces of duct tape.

With scrap posterboard, cut a circle about 3½ inches (9 cm) in diameter. Make a loop of duct tape, sticky side out, and use it to tape the

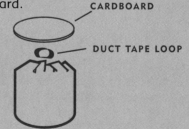

circle on top of the folded sections. Be sure to hide most of the tape.

Put on the hat. Pull the pillowcase on over the top of the hat so it hides most or all of the cardboard. Let the back of the pillowcase drape down your back. Have someone pin the excess hem behind the back of your neck.

Finish your outfit with lots of jewelry.

ACTIVITY

Simple Blackberry Dye

You can make a purple dye without snails by using blackberries. It's not permanent like the Phoenicians', but it's cheaper and not nearly as smelly. Note: This dyeing process takes about 3 hours. Don't wash the dyed socks with other clothes as the colors may run. Adult supervision is recommended.

Materials

Liquid dish soap

Large bowl or bucket

Warm water

1 or more pairs clean white socks; 100 percent cotton or wool works best

2 cups ripe blackberries (frozen or fresh)

Bowl and strainer for washing blackberries, if fresh

Large stainless steel pot

2 cups (480 ml) warm water

Stove

Large spoon

Tongs

Directions

Squirt a small amount of dish soap into the bowl or bucket. Fill it with warm water and add socks. Wash the socks, then let them soak in the soapy water for 30 minutes.

In the meantime, wash your berries (if fresh) and put them in the pot on the stove. Add about 2 cups (480 ml) warm water, or enough to completely cover them. Don't add too much water because it dilutes the dye.

After 30 minutes of soaking, rinse the socks thoroughly in warm water, wring them out, and put them—still damp—in the dye pot. Add enough water to barely cover the socks.

Cook your socks and berries on medium heat for an hour, stirring often. If the dye looks like it's about to boil, lower the heat to a simmer. Add water if needed to keep socks barely covered.

Let the socks cool in the dye for an hour. Stir them often.

With the tongs, transfer the socks from the pot to the bowl or bucket. Wash them with liquid soap and warm water. (Hot water will wash out too much dye.) Rinse with cool water until the water comes clear. Wring out the socks and hang them to dry.

Throw away the berries and dye.

The color will fade with time and washing. To make the color more permanent, you need to use a mordant (see "About Mordants" on page 62).

Becoming a Master Dyer

Like the Phoenicians, you can create a range of purplish hues by varying the dye ingredients, and dyeing and soaking times. Try using blueberries instead of blackberries, or mix the two. Try different amounts of water or berries. Add 1 to 3 teaspoons (5 to 15 ml) of white vinegar to change the color. You can also cook the dye longer or shorter amounts of time. For stronger colors, let the socks cool in the dye overnight. (Strain out the berries first, or they will leave splotches.)

Different fabrics produce different colors from the same dye. You'll get the brightest results with wool. Cotton and synthetic fibers will give paler colors, and polyester may not dye at all. Keep records and experiment.

Phoenician Language and Writing

Because the Phoenicians mostly wrote on papyrus, few of their writings have survived. But the Phoenicians left a legacy far more enduring: their alphabet. The Phoenician alphabet is the ancestor of the Israelites' and our own. Most scholars agree the Phoenicians spread the alphabet, but didn't invent it themselves. Who did? Read on for one possible answer.

Amazing Graffiti

In 1993, scholars came upon two mysterious messages scratched on cliffs in Egypt's Sinai desert. Some of the symbols looked like Egyptian hieroglyphs, but with a twist—each symbol stood for a single sound, not a word, syllable, or group of consonants. These writings—dated between 1900 and 1800 B.C.E.—used an alphabet. Scholars believe it is the oldest ancestor of the Phoenician alphabet found so far.

Although scholars cannot understand all the words, they believe the inscriptions are in a Semitic language—perhaps a language spoken by the ancient inhabitants of Canaan. Scholars think that Canaanites working for the Egyptians might have borrowed Egyptian symbols and used them in this new way.

In time, the Phoenicians learned a form of this early alphabet, simplified it, and ended up passing it to others. The Greeks learned it from the Phoenicians, changing it in the process.

The Romans learned it from the Greeks, changing it again. The English (among many others) learned it from the Romans, changing it still more. The letters on page 71 are the great-grandchildren of those used by Phoenicians so long ago.

The alphabet the Phoenicians used wasn't the only early alphabet. People in Ugarit, in Syria, invented a different alphabet based on cuneiform signs. If that one had caught on instead, we would all be using a different alphabet today.

The Phoenician Alphabet

Compare the Phoenician alphabet to the English alphabet. You'll notice it's quite different—but very similar to the Israelite alphabet on page 24. That's because the Israelites started by using the Phoenician alphabet, while many more steps separate the Phoenician alphabet from English.

Neither the Phoenician nor the Israelite alphabet used vowels, and both contained letters standing for sounds that don't exist in English, such as aleph, 'ayin, and khet.

The Alphabet: A Writing Revolution

Before the alphabet, most writing was done by specialists called scribes. Two main writing systems existed: hieroglyphic (hi-ro-GLIF-ic), invented in Egypt, and cuneiform (KYOON-ee-i-form), developed in Mesopotamia. In hieroglyphic writing, pictures called hieroglyphs (HI-ro-glifs) stood for words, consonants, or groups of consonants. In cuneiform, patterns of long thin triangles called wedges stood for syllables or words. Learning either system took years because of the number of symbols to memorize. Think how hard writing would be if you needed a different symbol for every syllable: BA, BE, BI, BO, BU, AB, EB, IB, OB, UB, BAB, BEB, BIB, and so on. Now imagine that some symbols also stood for words. Tricky, no?

With the invention of the alphabet, people needed only 20 to 30 letters instead of hundreds or thousands of signs. Because it was so much easier, some ordinary people began learning to read and write.

This form of the Phoenician alphabet was used on the tomb of King Ahiram around 1000 B.C.E. Because not every letter was used on his tomb, two letters—qoph and tsadi—come from another Phoenician inscription.

Possible Phoenician Letter Name	Ancient Phoenician Letter	Sound
Aleph	✵	Sound made in the throat
Bet	𓊪	B
Gimel	𐤂	G
Dalet	𐤃	D
Hey	𐤄	H
Waw	𐤅	W
Zayn	𐤆	Z
Khet	𐤇	Kh (like clearing the throat)
Tet	⊕	T
Yod	𐤉	Y
Kaph	𐤊	K

Possible Phoenician Letter Name	Ancient Phoenician Letter	Sound
Lamed	𐤋	L
Mem	𐤌	M
Nun	𐤍	N
Samek	𐤎	S
'Ayin	○	Sound deep in the throat
Pay	𐤐	P
Tsadi	𐤑	Ts
Qoph	Ø	Like K only pronounced deeper in the throat (pronounced like Kof)
Resh	𐤓	R
Shin	𐤔	Sh
Taw	+	T

ACTIVITY

Writing and Reading Like a Phoenician

Try writing a note to a friend using the Phoenician alphabet. Substitute Phoenician letters for English ones. Skip the vowels, since the Phoenicians didn't use them. Or, you can use "extra" letters to stand for vowels—letters that stood for sounds that don't exist in English, such as aleph, 'ayin, and khet. Decide what they stand for (maybe aleph for A, and 'ayin for E, I, and O), and tell your friend.

Now try reading the line below from a nursery rhyme. The sample below leaves out the vowels and uses tsadi ($\mathcal{L}$) instead of J, and pay ($\mathcal{I}$) instead of F or V. Remember to read from right to left!

taw   lamed hay   hay tet   pay   taw nun waw   lamed tsadi   dalet nun   kaph tsadi

.resh taw waw   pay   lamed pay   shin taw pay

This papyrus (and its ancient writing) are Egyptian. The Phoenicians may have imported the papyrus they used from Egypt. Courtesy of Scott Noegel.

Answer to nursery rhyme puzzle: Jack and Jill went up the hill to fetch a pail of water.

72

Phoenician Work

One important kind of Phoenician work was building boats and ships. Small Phoenician boats called hippoi, or "horses," by the Greeks, had fronts—and sometimes backs—shaped like horse's heads. Bigger Phoenician trading ships, called "tubs" because of their deep, rounded hulls, sailed the Mediterranean, carrying goods from land to land.

In the big trading ships, a single rectangular sail hung from a sturdy mast. Sailors raised and lowered the sail using ropes called brails, which worked like the cords on a mini-blind. By loosening these ropes, they could lower the sail into place when the wind was good for sailing. By tightening them, they could raise the sail and tuck it up and out of the way when a storm risked blowing the ship off course.

Sea Voyages and Trade

With their skillfully built ships, the Phoenicians became famous sea traders. Phoenician trading ships carried goods to and from Egypt, Syria, Canaan, and the island of Cyprus, as well as to other peoples great and small along the eastern Mediterranean.

They also traded between these lands and lands in Europe and northern Africa, including areas later called Spain, Malta, Sicily, Tunisia (too-NEE-zha), and Morocco. After some years of trade, they established colonies in these lands and others. Their most famous colony was Carthage, in what is now the North African nation of Tunisia.

The Phoenicians were famous for navigating (finding their way across the seas). They usually traveled within sight of land. At night, or when land wasn't visible, they set their course by a star. They sometimes traveled very far from home. The Greek historian Herodotus reported that Phoenicians once sailed around all of Africa. So dangerous was this journey that no one repeated it for thousands of years. Is this story true? Many historians think it probably is.

Two kinds of Phoenician ships carried the people of Tyre to safety when the Assyrians attacked—trading ships and warships. The trading ships had raised fronts and backs, while the warships had pointed fronts and curved backs. Here, only the warships are shown with masts. Notice the tall headdresses of Phoenician women. Courtesy of Sir Austen Henry Layard, from an Assyrian carving in the British Museum. © The British Museum.

What Did the Phoenicians Trade?

Many of the goods the Phoenicians carried were made in Phoenician cities. These goods included small, fragile bottles of bright-colored glass; dyed purple cloth; carved ivory panels for cedar furniture; and pendants, earrings, bracelets, and other ornaments. Wine and oil, produced in other lands, were bottled in clay Phoenician jars and sent abroad. In exchange, the Phoenician traders brought back silver, copper, and tin from Spain, Italy, ancient Turkey, and Cyprus; gold from Spain and Africa; linen from Egypt; and olive oil and wheat from ancient Israel.

This silver bowl shows animals and designs that stand for trees. In the middle, a being with four wings attacks a lion. Courtesy of The Metropolitan Museum of Art, The Cesnola Collection. Purchased by subscription, 1874–76. (74.51.4554).

ACTIVITY

Decorated Cup or Bowl

The Phoenicians were famous for making decorated bowls of silver, gold, or bronze. They hammered the sides into small molds, to create rows of decorations such as flowers, people, and animals. Some of the pictures tell stories of hunts or war. You can decorate a cup or bowl to look a bit like theirs.

Materials

Newspaper or other table protection

Blunt pencil or paintbrush

Styrofoam cup or bowl

Acrylic or tempera paint, copper or silver colored

4 cotton balls

Jar of water

Directions

Look at the picture of the decorated bowl and plan your design.

Spread newspaper on your work surface. Fold several sheets into fourths for a palette.

Using the pencil or the handle end of a paintbrush, scratch your design onto the styrofoam. Be careful not to pierce the styrofoam.

Decorate the inside of a bowl, or the outside of a cup. Squeeze a little paint on the palette. Try mixing silver and copper to look like bronze.

Use the cotton ball to spread the paint smoothly over the decorated surface of the styrofoam. If you apply it thickly, the lines on the cup will stand out darker. If you apply it lightly, your lines will appear white. Decide which style you like best.

If you want, paint the other surface (outside or inside) of your cup or bowl.

Display your finished piece as art, but don't use it for food or drink.

ACTIVITY

Model Trading Ship

Make a model trading ship with a sail you can open and close. This can be a tricky project; it is best suited for experienced craft-makers. Allow several days between Part I and Part II to let the ship dry.

Part I: Making the Hull (ship's body)

Materials

- Newspaper or other table protection
- Newspaper for papier-mâché
- Clean, empty, 2-liter soda bottle (save the cap)
- Scissors
- Masking tape
- Several pieces of foil, each 12 inches (30 cm) square
- 1½ cups (360 ml) flour
- 3 cups (720 ml) water
- Small bowl
- Spoon or fork for mixing
- Paper towels
- Toilet paper tube

Directions

Spread some newspaper on the table, and tear the rest of it into long strips for papier-mâché.

Cut the soda bottle in half the long way, making two ship-shaped objects. The bottle bottom is too thick to cut, so cut up and around it, leaving it attached to one half of the bottle. Cut off and discard the spout, but save the cap. Use the bottle half with the bottom attached and discard the other half.

Cover the sharp edges of the bottle with masking tape.

Model a prow and stern (front and back of the ship) from aluminum foil. To do this, fold layers of foil over and over to make two flat rectangular foil shapes about 6 inches (15 cm) long and 2 to 3 inches (5 to 7.5 cm) wide. Bend each in the middle, forming two "L" shapes. Turn an L upside-down and tape it inside one end of the ship. The bent-over part should stick out past the ship body, parallel to the table. Repeat this procedure on the other end.

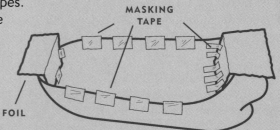

MASKING TAPE

FOIL

77

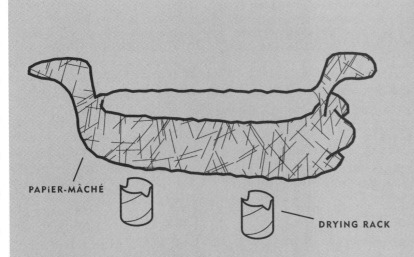

PAPIER-MÂCHÉ

DRYING RACK

Part II: Completing the Ship

Materials

Newspaper or other table protection

Dry hull from Part I

Cardboard (backing from a notepad works well)

Pen or pencil

Scissors

Thick cardboard or scrap wood, large enough to set the hull upon

Large needle with large eye

Small and large nails

Wooden chopstick (large size with square end is best)

Bottle cap from Part I

Non-hardening modeling clay, enough for a ball about 1 inch (2.5 cm) in diameter

Duct tape

Acrylic or tempera paints

Paintbrushes

Jar of water

Drying rack from Part I

10-inch-long (25-cm) wooden skewer or thin stick

Scotch tape

12 inches (30 cm) string

White felt, about 6 by 8½ inches (15 x 21 cm)

Stapler

4 16-inch (40-cm) pieces of embroidery floss

Mix ½ cup (120 ml) of flour with 1 cup (240 ml) of water in small bowl. (Mix more as needed.) Dip in strips of paper, smooth off excess paste with your fingers, and apply 2 to 3 layers of papier-mâché to the inside and outside of the ship, arranging the layers in criss-cross fashion. (Apply the first layer of strips the long way, and the second layer the short way, for example.) Fill in the bumps on the bottom of the bottle with extra strips. Shape the prow and stern into their final forms. If necessary, make more paste with the remaining flour and water.

Make a drying rack by cutting the toilet paper tube in half to create two short tubes. In the end of one tube, cut two small V-shaped notches across from each other (both on the same end). Repeat this procedure with the other half tube. Set the hull onto the notches to dry. Save this drying rack for later use.

Directions

Spread newspaper on the table.

Turn the hull upside down, hold it still, and trace around the deck onto the cardboard. Cut it out and trim the two ends so that the deck will fit easily on top of the hull. Remove the deck from the hull.

Draw a dot in the exact middle of the deck. Put the thick cardboard or scrap wood underneath the deck and poke a hole through the dot with the needle. Use the nails to make this hole larger. Carefully slide the chopstick—the mast—through the hole, starting with the narrow end, until all but 2 to 3 inches (5 to 7.5 cm) of chopstick have slid through. The chopstick should fit tightly into the hole.

CLAY ———

BOTTLE CAP———

DUCT TAPE
WITH FRINGES———
UNDER CAP

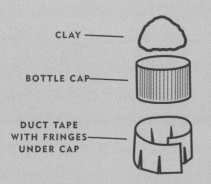

Mound the bottle cap with clay. Place the bottle cap on the table, flat side down, and stick the broad end of the chopstick (with the deck attached) into the clay. With the mast, cap, and deck attached, place the bottle cap inside the hull and arrange the deck in place. Slide the deck up the mast without moving the bottle cap. Draw around the cap, marking its place inside the hull. Unstick the mast from the clay. Make a small loop of duct tape, sticky side out, and use this to attach the underside of the cap to the hull at the spot you marked. Now cut a 1- to 2-inch (2.5- to 5-cm) piece of duct tape and cut fringes along one side. Wrap the unfringed part around the edge of the bottle cap so the fringed part sticks to the hull. (Don't cover the clay.) Repeat this step until the cap is well fastened to the hull bottom.

Paint the hull, inside and out. Phoenician ships were often black. Paint the duct tape but not the clay or the deck. Set the hull on the drying rack to dry.

Make the sail support. Carefully remove the mast from the deck. Lay the skewer crosswise about 1 inch (2.5 cm) from narrow tip of the mast. Attach tightly with scotch tape. Replace it in the deck to test the position of the sail support. (The sail will hang from it, and should face the front of the ship.) Remove the support from the deck and reinforce the tape by tying the pieces together with string, looping it in figure eights and tying tightly. Trim the skewer with scissors if the sides are uneven.

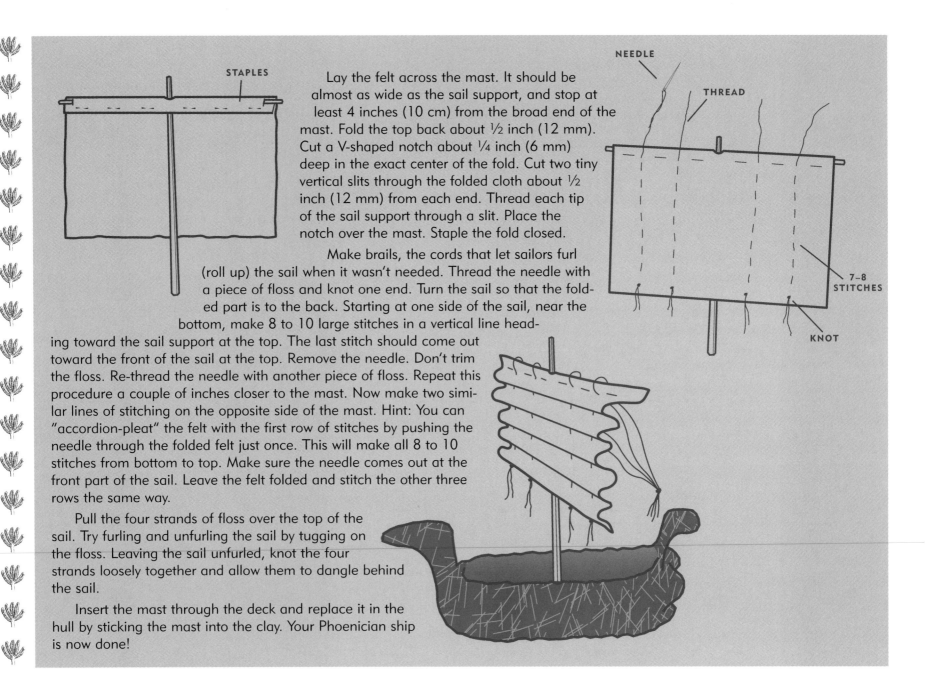

Lay the felt across the mast. It should be almost as wide as the sail support, and stop at least 4 inches (10 cm) from the broad end of the mast. Fold the top back about ½ inch (12 mm). Cut a V-shaped notch about ¼ inch (6 mm) deep in the exact center of the fold. Cut two tiny vertical slits through the folded cloth about ½ inch (12 mm) from each end. Thread each tip of the sail support through a slit. Place the notch over the mast. Staple the fold closed.

Make brails, the cords that let sailors furl (roll up) the sail when it wasn't needed. Thread the needle with a piece of floss and knot one end. Turn the sail so that the folded part is to the back. Starting at one side of the sail, near the bottom, make 8 to 10 large stitches in a vertical line heading toward the sail support at the top. The last stitch should come out toward the front of the sail at the top. Remove the needle. Don't trim the floss. Re-thread the needle with another piece of floss. Repeat this procedure a couple of inches closer to the mast. Now make two similar lines of stitching on the opposite side of the mast. Hint: You can "accordion-pleat" the felt with the first row of stitches by pushing the needle through the folded felt just once. This will make all 8 to 10 stitches from bottom to top. Make sure the needle comes out at the front part of the sail. Leave the felt folded and stitch the other three rows the same way.

Pull the four strands of floss over the top of the sail. Try furling and unfurling the sail by tugging on the floss. Leaving the sail unfurled, knot the four strands loosely together and allow them to dangle behind the sail.

Insert the mast through the deck and replace it in the hull by sticking the mast into the clay. Your Phoenician ship is now done!

Phoenician Food

The rich farmlands of Phoenicia produced many harvests: grapes, olives, other fruits and vegetables, and grain. Mainland farmers sent fruit, vegetables, wheat, and barley to the Phoenician cities, and raised sheep and goats for milk and meat. Fish teemed in the coastal waters, providing food for the Phoenicians' tables and for trade. Ancient people probably ate many other foods in common with modern Lebanese, including cucumbers, herbs, and yogurt—a way to preserve milk without a refrigerator.

Food for Export

Phoenician ships carried fish, grain, wine, oil, and chopped meat preserved in wine to ports near and far. Usually they shipped them in amphorae (am-FOR-ay)—large clay jars with pointed bottoms.

Cucumbers in Yogurt Sauce

Cucumbers in yogurt sauce are eaten throughout the Near East today.
Modern Lebanese call this dish "Khiar Bil-Laban" (KHEE-ar bil la-BAN).
Adult supervision is recommended.

Ingredients

1 cucumber

2 cups (480 ml) plain yogurt

½ (2.5 ml) teaspoon minced garlic or
⅛ (0.5 ml) teaspoon garlic powder

1 tablespoon (15 ml) dried mint (mint
from a peppermint tea bag works well)

1 teaspoon (5 ml) salt

Utensils

Cutting board

Vegetable peeler

Knife

Medium-sized bowl

Measuring cup

Measuring spoons

Spoon

Directions

Wash your hands.

Rinse the cucumber.

Peel it by pushing the peeler away from you. Carefully slice it and cut each slice into a couple of bite-size pieces.

Put the cucumber in the bowl and add yogurt.

Add the garlic, salt, and mint. Stir thoroughly.

Serve cold.

Famous Fish Sauce

One famous Phoenician delicacy was garum (GA-rum), a sauce of fermented fish. Layers of fish (guts and all) would sit in a clay container for months, separated by layers of salt and other seasonings. You can imagine how it smelled! In time, a clear liquid rose to the top. The Phoenicians would use that liquid—garum—for flavoring.

It's not clear when the Phoenicians began eating garum, but it was eaten for generations all around the Mediterranean. The modern food it most resembles is a fish sauce eaten in Vietnam and Thailand. Some food historians believe that long ago, the Vietnamese and Thai people got the idea for fish sauce from the Romans, who learned it from the Phoenicians.

ACTIVITY

Model Amphora

Make a model amphora. Allow a few days for drying between steps.

Part I: Making the Amphora

Materials

- Newspapers or other table protection
- ¼ pound (115 g) Celluclay (artificial papier-mâché), or use real papier-mâché, from page 77
- Bowl
- Water
- Spoon
- 2 sheets of waxed paper or plastic wrap, each about 18 inches (45 cm) long
- Rolling pin or large, smooth glass jar
- Disposable plastic drinking cup with mouth wider than base
- Scissors
- 500 ml (1 pint) plastic water bottle with flat, round cap
- Several inches (approximately 10 cm) of aluminum foil

Directions

Spread newspaper on the table.

Mix Celluclay according to the package directions.

Place a handful of Celluclay onto one sheet of the waxed paper or plastic wrap. Cover with the second sheet. Roll the clay flat with a jar or rolling pin.

Make a stand for the bottle by cutting the bottom from the plastic cup. Place the bottle in the upside-down cup.

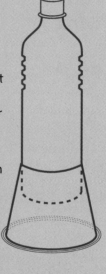

Wrap a thin layer of Celluclay around the bottle, avoiding the bottleneck near the cap.

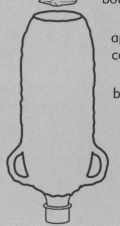

Continue rolling out and applying the Celluclay until the sides of the bottle are covered. Don't cover the bottom yet.

Make two handles out of Celluclay. Attach just below the bottleneck.

Shape the foil into a small solid cone. Place the cone on the bottom of bottle, pointing out. Cover the cone and the rest of the base with Celluclay.

Let the bottle dry. Drying will take 2 to 3 days. Save the stand for Part II.

ACTIVITY

Part II: Painting the Amphora

Materials

Newspaper or other table protection

Dry bottle with lid from Part I

Stand made from plastic cup

Acrylic paints, red-brown for a historical look or any color desired

Paintbrushes

Jar of water

Optional: Modge-podge glue or white acrylic medium (available in art or craft stores).

Directions

Spread newspapers on the table.

Balance the bottle on the stand or on its cap that has no papier-mâché.

Paint the entire bottle, except the area just around the cap.

Let dry for about 45 minutes. Meanwhile, wash the brushes.

Optional: To help protect the bottle from water damage, coat it with Modge-podge or acrylic medium. Let dry again.

When the outside is dry, you can fill the bottle with water. Even with the coating, water can still damage the outside, so don't try to wash it. Display the finished bottle by leaning it against a wall, or balancing it in the stand you made.

This amphora (most likely used for shipping wine) was recovered from a Phoenician shipwreck nicknamed "Tanit" (for a goddess of the Phoenicians) that sank sometime between 750 and 700 B.C.E. Courtesy of WHO, IFE, Ashkelon Excavations; Photo by Carl Andrew.

Phoenician Religion

Like most people in the ancient Near East, the Phoenicians didn't worship a single God. Instead, they worshipped many gods and goddesses. Some of their gods shared the names of deities worshipped elsewhere in the region: goddesses Astarte and Asherah, and gods El and Baal. People of different cities worshipped different forms of these deities. For example, the people of Tyre worshipped Baal Shamem, who was different from other Baals worshipped in other places. Each city had a special god and goddess that protected it, and each family had its own special gods as well, often ancestors. In addition, the Phoenicians worshipped Eshmun (esh-MOON), the god of healing, and other deities, including some Egyptian gods.

Although Phoenician temples were probably small, they had large staffs: priestesses and priests, servants, musicians, singers, dancers, barbers, butchers, and bakers. These people performed rituals, prepared animals and baked goods for sacrifice, shaved the priests' heads, and entertained the gods and goddesses with music and dance. Members of the city's royal family served as the most important priests.

Children growing up in Phoenicia learned the importance of keeping the gods happy. Gods could become angry if they weren't worshipped correctly, and they might cause untold damage—plague, shipwreck, drought, or defeat in battle. When this happened, the priests would try to appease the gods with even more sacrifices and rituals. When things went well, people showed their thanks by burning incense and offering delicacies such as milk, wine, honey, fruit, oil, bread, cakes, or perfume, which they sometimes threw into sacred pools.

The Mystery of the Masks

In Phoenician tombs and some places of worship, archaeologists have uncovered clay masks with cut-out eyes and mouths. Some masks were large enough for adults to wear, but many were child-size or smaller. Usually these masks depicted men, often with long beards and curled hair. Were these masks meant to be worn in rituals? Did the Phoenicians put the smaller ones on statues of their gods? No one knows for sure.

Child Sacrifice

Except for a few inscriptions on gravestones or coffins, no records of Phoenician religion have survived. Scholars must rely on archaeology and on records from other cultures—often the Phoenicians' enemies. Sometimes scholars disagree about how to interpret this evidence. One big question has to do with a monstrous practice: child sacrifice.

The Greeks, Romans, and Israelites all accused the Phoenicians of sacrificing babies to their gods. In some Phoenician colonies,

Still carrying the remains of paint, this clay mask of a man was found in an Iron-Age cemetery.
Courtesy of the Israel Antiquities Authority.

ACTIVITY

Phoenician Mask

You can make a "mystery mask" like the Phoenicians' that you can hang on your wall.

Materials

- Newspaper or other table protection
- Potter's clay or self-drying clay such as Marblex, about 2 cups (480 ml)
- Disposable oval-shaped microwave-safe container
- Skewer or nail
- Old table knife
- Strong cord for hanging

Directions

Spread newspaper on the table.

CUT OUT

Knead the clay for several minutes to help prevent cracking when it dries. Thwack and pound it firmly.

Turn the microwave container upside down. Mold the clay mask on top of it. You can let the mask's edges hang slightly over the sides of the container. Do not entirely cover the container's sides, or the mask may crack when you remove it. If you are making a mask of a man, include hair, nose, lips, ears, and a beard. With the knife, cut out eye-shaped holes, and perhaps the mouth.

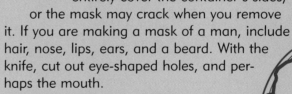

Poke a small round hole near the top of the mask, big enough to string a cord through.

Allow several days to dry. When the mask is dry, remove from the container, loop a short strong cord through the hole, knot firmly, and hang on a hook or nail.

archaeologists have found burial grounds filled with the burnt bones of babies. Inscriptions say the babies were offered to a goddess called Tanit (ta-NEET) or sometimes to a god named Baal Hammon.

Archaeologists call these burial grounds tophets (TOE-fets). The name comes from a spot mentioned in the Bible, near Jerusalem. According to the Bible, some Israelites used to sacrifice their children there as offerings to a god named Moloch (MA-lukh), until King Josiah stopped them.

Although no tophets have been found in the Phoenician homeland, many scholars suspect child sacrifice was practiced there, too.

How could parents possibly sacrifice their child? The Greek and Roman historians—disgusted by the practice—claim that Phoenicians did it when their city was imperiled by plague or war. Inscriptions on some gravestones suggest otherwise. Some parents may have sacrificed their babies in return for a favor from a goddess or god.

But some historians think the Phoenicians were innocent. They believe that the babies in the graveyards died from other causes, such as illness. (In ancient times, babies often died from illnesses that doctors can treat or prevent today.) According to these historians, only after the baby had already died would the parents offer the child as a sacrifice to the gods. What do you think? Did the Phoenicians really kill their babies? What kinds of information would help you decide?

The God Who Rose from the Dead

Tyre's chief god was named Melqart, which is Phoenician for "King of the City." In the minds of the people of Tyre, Melqart ruled over plant life, the sea, and even the underworld, where the dead were supposed to go. His goddess-wife Astarte helped people and animals become pregnant and have babies.

The people of Tyre believed that Melqart died each winter and came back to life each spring, just like the plants he ruled. According to the ancient historian Josephus, near each winter's end, the Phoenicians symbolized the god's death by setting his image on fire. In a later ceremony they celebrated his rebirth and marriage.

Conclusion

The Phoenicians' history—and their influence—didn't end with the Iron Age. Their most famous colony, Carthage, continued to wield power long after the period covered in this book. Carthage, in Africa, established its own trading empire and its own colonies around the Mediterranean. Between 510 and 279 B.C.E., it allied itself with Rome to battle the Greeks, its rivals in trade. Later, Rome and Carthage fought each other, mostly at sea. Then, in 218 B.C.E., a Carthaginian general named Hannibal (HAN-i-bal) did something never done before in the history of the world: he crossed two mountain ranges in Europe with his army and a group of war elephants. Although he won many battles, in the end Rome was the victor. Hannibal went into exile and killed himself to keep from being handed over to the Romans. After still another war, in 146 B.C.E., Rome destroyed Carthage.

We hear little of the Phoenicians today. Yet these ancient traders played an enormous role in shaping our world. They brought knowledge and skills from the eastern Mediterranean to the west. Their powerful ships served as models for their enemies, the Greeks and Romans, to use. Some of their colonies, like Cadiz in Spain, developed into cities that survive today. Their influence extends into our daily life as well. If you eat Thai or Vietnamese food, you may be eating the descendant of Phoenician fish sauce. In fact, you are experiencing the influence of their alphabet this very moment, just by reading this book. If the Phoenicians had not lived, our world would be a very different place.

PART 3

THE PHILISTINES

Israel, Phoenicia, and Philistia during the Iron Age.

Philistine History

Around 1175 B.C.E., as the Israelites were settling in Canaan's hill country, newcomers called the "Sea Peoples" arrived on Canaan's southern shores. One Sea People, the Philistines, became the Israelites' most famous enemy. Today the word "Philistine" is an insult meaning uncultured—lacking appreciation for art and beauty. Who were the Philistines? Where did they come from? Do they deserve their bad reputation? Read on, and see what you think.

Who Were the Philistines?

For centuries, scholars knew little about the Philistines except what was in the Bible. (See "Samson and Delilah" and "David and the Philistines" for two of the most famous Bible stories.) Then, in 1821, a French scholar—Jean François Champollion (shom-po-lee-AWN)—deciphered carvings on the walls of a temple of Ramses III (RAM-zeez the third) in the ancient Egyptian city of Thebes. In these carvings, Egyptians battled foreigners, including one group they may have called the "Peleset," on land and sea. (The exact Egyptian pronunciation isn't known for sure.) These "Peleset" were the Philistines.

Carvings on an Egyptian temple show Philistine prisoners, captured in a long-ago battle in Egypt a few years before the Philistines entered Canaan.
Courtesy of Scott Noegel.

In these and other records, the Egyptians claimed to have bested the Philistines and other Sea Peoples, including the Sherden, Denyen, and Sikils (sometimes called the Tjekker). According to records of Ramses III, the Egyptians captured some of the Sea Peoples and settled them in forts, probably in 1175 B.C.E. Some scholars believe these forts were on Canaan's southern coast, and that this is how the Philistines arrived in Canaan. (The Egyptians controlled much of Canaan before the Sea Peoples arrived, but withdrew soon after to handle problems at home.) Other scholars believe the Sea Peoples settled in Canaan on their own.

The Sikils settled north of the Philistines. (The Story of Wen-Amun, on page 52 of the Phoenician section, describes the Sikils through the eyes of an Egyptian priest.) The Sherden probably settled still farther north, around the northern part of modern Israel.

According to the Bible, the Philistines built five capital cities on the coast of Canaan: Ashdod, Ashkelon, Ekron, Gaza, and Gath. In the past 80 years, archaeologists have unearthed three—possibly four—of these. They now know the Philistines created beautiful pottery, strong and well-planned

In a carving from Ramses III's temple in Egypt, Egyptian soldiers battle Sea Peoples warriors on board ships. The Egyptians wear straight, dark wigs. Tall, feathered headdresses adorn the Philistines' heads, while another Sea People— the Sherden—wear helmets with horns. Courtesy of the Israel Exploration Society.

Samson and Delilah

In a famous Bible story, Philistine leaders used trickery to defeat Samson, an Israelite warrior and judge with superhuman strength. The Philistines bribed Samson's girlfriend Delilah to tell them how they could weaken him. She told them Samson's secret: cut his hair and he'd lose his strength. With Delilah's help, the Philistines bound Samson while he slept, then shaved his hair off. He awoke to find himself their prisoner. The Philistines chained him between two pillars in their temple so they could mock him. Praying to God to return his strength one last time, Samson thrust the pillars apart. The temple roof collapsed, killing Samson along with hundreds of Philistines.

cities, and objects of iron and bronze. Still, mysteries remain. The biggest mystery is where the Philistines and the other Sea Peoples came from.

The Philistines arrived in Canaan when the ancient world was in chaos. Great civilizations were toppling all around the eastern Mediterranean and Aegean (a-JEE-un) Seas. (The Aegean Sea lay northwest of Canaan, partly bordered by the Greek mainland and islands on the west, and the coast of Anatolia—ancient Turkey—on the east.) Groups of people were traveling by ship or land from one city to another, both fleeing the chaos and helping create it. Some groups became pirates and attacked and looted cities and ships. Some merely sought a new home.

The Sea Peoples who settled in Canaan were part of this massive migration. But where was their first home? Archaeologists have been tracking clues: painted decorations on pots; remains of their diet, including piles of pig bones; their style of architecture. Scholars have looked throughout the ancient world for other artifacts matching these. Over and over, they have found them in two places: the island of Cyprus and the area around the Aegean. Scholars agree that Cyprus was probably not the Philistines' first home. Most scholars believe they came from the Aegean area.

The Philistines over Time

When the Philistines first settled on Canaan's coast, they conquered a number of Canaanite cities and set up some brand-new settlements as well. Ruling over many of the local Canaanite people, they expanded their territory north, south, and east. By about 1000 B.C.E., they were probably the strongest group in Canaan.

At first, the Philistines kept many customs from their homeland. But as the centuries passed, they took on parts of their neighbors' culture. They began speaking a related language, and adopted an alphabet like their neighbors'. They probably came to worship some Canaanite gods.

Around 734 B.C.E. the Assyrians defeated the Philistines. In the following years, they demanded the Philistines pay them tribute, and sometimes chose the Philistines' kings. At least once, the Philistines allied with the Israelites and other kingdoms to try to defeat the Assyrians. They lost.

Under the Assyrians, Philistine cities grew in size and wealth. The Assyrians encouraged each city to develop its own special industry—olive oil, pottery, or wine. Then the Assyrians left to tend to problems in their own land. Briefly, the Egyptians took control. Finally, King Nebuchadnezzar of Babylonia—the same king who burned Jerusalem—destroyed all of the Philistine cities just before 600 B.C.E. After that, Philistine culture came to an end.

Were the Philistines "Philistines"?

Because of their reputation in the Bible, the word "Philistine" (sometimes with a small *p*) has a special meaning in English. If you recall, it means someone who doesn't appreciate art or beauty. But archaeology paints a different picture of these people. The Philistines had a sophisticated culture. Their pottery was much finer than the Israelites'. They established well-ordered cities while most Israelites lived in small, rough settlements. Perhaps it's time we stopped looking at the Philistines through their enemies' eyes. Were the Philistines "philistines"? What do you think?

David and the Philistines

The Bible describes about 150 years of battles between the Philistines and the Israelites, beginning around Samson's time. As the Philistine threat grew, the Israelites demanded a king to help them. But the Philistines defeated the Israelites' first king, Saul.

The most famous Bible story about the Philistines took place during Saul's reign. In this story, a young Israelite named David defeated the Philistine champion, a heavily armed, boastful giant named Goliath (go-LIE-ath). David used no sword or armor, only a slingshot and five smooth stones. But these weapons were more than enough. Aiming his first stone at Goliath's forehead, David felled the giant, then used Goliath's own sword to chop off his head. Later David went on to become the Israelites' second—and most famous—king.

As king, David won important victories over the Philistines. They didn't go away, but they became much less of a threat to the Israelites after that.

Philistine Architecture

ost Philistines were city-dwellers. They built cities with strong walls and good planning. Their cities had separate sections for living and working, and another section for public buildings, temples, and rich people's homes.

Archaeologists have unearthed three of the large Philistine cities named in the Bible—Ashdod, Ekron, and Ashkelon—and another that might be Gath, Goliath's hometown. They've also dug up smaller settlements such as Beth Shemesh and Tell Qasile (tel ka-SEE-lay).

Among the ruins, archaeologists have sought clues to the Philistines' homeland. Some think they have found such a clue in a special kind of hearth.

Hearths and Homelands

Today, we usually think of hearths in front of fireplaces. Ancient hearths, however, often stood alone, without a fireplace or chimney. People built their fires directly on the hearths. Philistine hearths often appeared in the middle of courtyards.

In Greece and Cyprus, large households and palaces sometimes held long assembly rooms with huge hearths in the middle. Thrones for the lord and lady of the house stood nearby. Pillars supported the ceiling, and elaborate murals decorated the walls. No such hearth rooms have been found in ancient Israel. But some archaeologists believe they've identified two

This is how a hearth room in an ancient Greek palace might have looked.
Courtesy of the Department of Classics, University of Cincinnati.

A(TIVITY

Model Hearth Room

You can make a model Aegean hearth room. Make it as elegant as you like. We don't know if the Philistines really had rooms like this, but it's fun to imagine they did.

Materials

Newspaper or other table protection

Shoebox (no lid)

Jar or lid for tracing around

Pencil

White glue

Paintbrush

Handful of tiny pebbles

3 pieces of white or colored construction paper

Scissors

Markers or paints and paintbrushes

2 to 4 note cards or 1 piece of posterboard (more is optional)

Scotch tape

Optional: model people

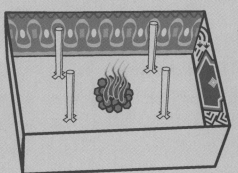

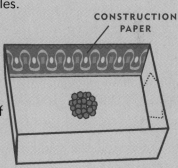

PEBBLES

CONSTRUCTION PAPER

Directions

Spread newspaper on the table.

Place the jar or lid in the middle of the inside of the box. Trace around it.

Squeeze glue inside the circle and spread it with the brush. Cover the circle with pebbles.

Trace around each side of the shoebox onto the construction paper (use the outside of the box). Decorate the paper with brightly colored geometric designs or pictures of plants and animals. Be sure to draw a doorway. Trim pieces to fit inside the walls. Glue or tape on.

Make 2 to 4 pillars by rolling tubes of posterboard or note cards (lined side in) the long way.

Use tape to secure the tubes. The tubes should be slightly taller than the height of the box. Cut 4 slits in the bottom of each tube and splay the sides out. Tape the splayed-out pieces to the floor around the hearth.

If you like, build benches around the walls or build two thrones, side by side. Make the furniture by folding and taping colored or white posterboard.

Use colored construction paper to make a fake fire in the center of the hearth.

Put model people into your hearth room if you like.

hearths in the middle of rooms in Philistine buildings. One building is probably a temple, and the other probably a palace. The hearths were paved with pebbles and bits of broken pottery.

These Philistine rooms were smaller and simpler than the Greek hearth rooms. We don't know if decorations adorned the walls. Both of the Philistine rooms had pillars; one room had plaster-covered benches lining the walls.

Did these Philistine buildings reflect Aegean traditions? Many archaeologists believe they did. These scholars note that the Philistines rebuilt these rooms more than once as years went by. Each time, they made the hearth smaller. Then came a time when they left the hearths out entirely. Some archaeologists think they were losing touch with their Aegean roots.

Later Cities

Between 1000 and 900 B.C.E., the Israelites (or someone else) burned many Philistine cities. The Philistines rebuilt the cities not long after, but made them smaller. After the Assyrians gained control of the Philistines, some of these cities grew large once more, beginning around 701 B.C.E. However, they were never enormous. Ashkelon, one of the best-known of the Philistine cities, probably held 10,000 to 12,000 people when the Babylonians destroyed it around 604 B.C.E. Modern Washington, D.C., is about 50 times bigger!

Under the Assyrians, the Philistines erected many buildings. Large new storehouses, palaces, and temples went up. The city of Ekron was rebuilt and reorganized. In its industrial area, archaeologists uncovered dozens of workshops for making olive oil.

The Philistines generally fortified their cities. In 604 B.C.E., Ashkelon's walls bristled with as many as 50 towers. A steep slope outside the walls made it hard for attackers to reach the walls. But despite such defenses, the Philistine cities fell again and again. The power of the Assyrians, Egyptians, and Babylonians was too great for the Philistines to withstand.

Philistine Clothing

ew pictures exist that show what most Philistines wore. We know what Philistine soldiers wore from wall carvings on a temple in Egypt.

Military Style

The pictures on the temple of Pharaoh Ramses III show Egyptian soldiers clashing with warriors from the Sea Peoples on land and sea, around 1175 B.C.E. The soldiers of the Sea Peoples (all men) wore belted kilts (skirts) of cloth or leather, with tassels dangling from points on the hem. Some wore sleeveless or short-sleeved shirts with armor over their upper chests. They hoisted long spears and large round shields.

The most interesting part of their costume was the headdress. Pictures of the Philistines, Denyen, and Sikils—three groups of Sea Peoples—showed men wearing tall feathered headdresses with chinstraps. Other warriors of the Sea Peoples—the Sherden—wore round helmets with horns jutting out to either side. (See page 94.)

Other battle scenes showed women and children of the Sea Peoples in carts pulled by oxen. They were probably fleeing the fighting. The women had long hair or head scarves and long straight dresses. The children may have been naked. (It's hard to see the details on the wall carvings.)

Over time, did the military outfits change? The Bible describes the Philistine giant Goliath, at least 200 years later, wearing a bronze helmet, a heavy coat of mail, and bronze protectors on his legs. This outfit sounds different from the pictures of warriors carved by the Egyptians, but the Bible doesn't give very complete information. We don't know whether Goliath wore a kilt like the early Philistines or not. All we really know is that his clothes must have been extra-extra large!

Carvings on a temple of the Egyptian king Ramses III show Philistine prisoners wearing tall feathered head-dresses and kilts. Courtesy of the Israel Exploration Society.

ACTIVITY

Warrior's Headdress

You can make a headdress with "feathers" like those worn by early Philistine soldiers.
It's easier if a friend helps with the measuring.

Materials

Tape measure or string

Pencil

Thin posterboard, any color, at least 24 inches (60 cm) wide, wide enough to go around your head plus 2 inches (5 cm)

Optional: yardstick or meterstick

Scissors

Markers or paints

Brushes

Jar of water

4 sheets construction or thinner craft paper, 12 by 18 inches (30 x 45 cm), in 2 different colors

Tape

Stapler

Fabric strip or cloth ribbon, about 1 inch wide and 2 feet long (2.5 x 60 cm)

Directions

To make the headband, measure around your head with the tape measure or string. Mark the distance with a pencil on the posterboard then add 2 inches (5 cm). Cut a thin, 2-inch-wide (5 cm) strip of posterboard this length. (A yardstick will help you draw a straight line before cutting.) Decorate one side using markers or paints. You can use the picture of the Philistine headdress for ideas. (See page xviii.)

To make the feathers, cut a long strip of colored paper 3 to 4 inches (7.5 to 10 cm) wide. Cut fringes along one side of the strip. Fringes should be about 2 inches (5 cm) long. Tape the bottom of this strip along the back of the headband so that the bottom of the strip is about one-third up the headband and the fringes stick over the top. Cut another strip of the same color, if needed, so the entire headband has a fringe above it.

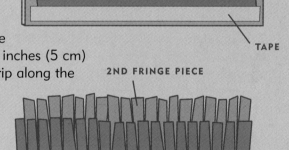

103

Now cut a second paper fringe in a different color. Tape it to the first strip about an inch higher.

Place the band around your head so it sits directly over your eyebrows to measure the size. Take it off, staple it into a ring with the staples pointing out, and put it back on. With your hand, smooth the fringes outward several times so they lean out over the headband.

To make the chinstrap, hold the fabric strip or ribbon under your chin. Allow at least an inch extra on either side to attach it to the headband and a little extra room so you can take your headdress on and off. Cut the strap the right length. Decorate it with paints or markers if desired. Before stapling it to the headband, hold it in position and draw around each end onto the outside of the headband. (This step is easier if you have a friend to help you.) Take off the headdress and mark similar spots inside the headband. Staple on the chinstrap at these inside outlines, with the staples pointing out.

Now put on your headdress and look fierce.

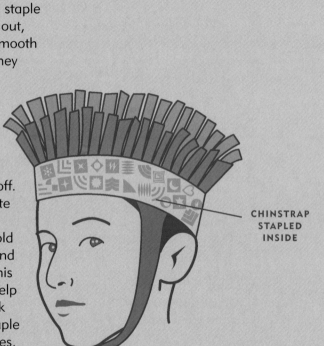

STAPLES

CHINSTRAP STAPLED INSIDE

Spinning and Weaving

In ancient times, making a garment took months of work: first making and weaving the thread (the slow part), then stitching the actual garment (the fast part). Because making cloth took so long, people probably used garments over and over—first as clothing, then as washcloths, bandages, potholders, and finally as rags—until the cloth fell apart completely.

In Philistine cities, archaeologists have unearthed parts of spindles—hand tools for making thread or yarn—like those used by peoples all across the region. Thousands of years ago, Philistine women and girls used these for hours at a time to twist wool into yarn. Although spinning took skill, girls probably learned to do it when they were quite young.

To weave cloth, the Philistines probably used two kinds of looms. One kind lay along the ground. In the biblical story of Samson and Delilah, Delilah wove Samson's long hair into a loom like this while he slept, so the Philistines could capture him. (Samson's hair was still attached to his head at the time.) When she woke him, he jumped up, breaking apart the loom. He escaped the Philistines that time, but he probably had a very sore scalp!

The Philistines also used upright looms, like other peoples in the region. Weavers tied lengths of thread to a beam of wood running along the top. To pull these threads taut, they tied weights to their ends. Then they wove other threads over and under the hanging threads to make cloth.

Archaeologists are interested in Philistine loom weights because some of them looked like weights used in Cyprus and the Aegean world. These loom weights looked like large clay peanuts, instead of the doughnut-shaped weights used by other peoples in their new home.

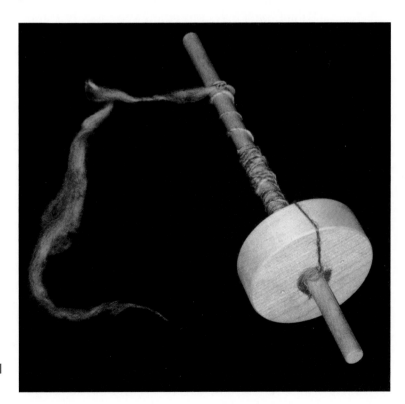

This modern spindle is all wood. Philistine spindles had a stick attached to a stone or clay disk.

ACTIVITY

Simple Spinning

You can try the simplest kind of spinning. You won't use a spindle—just your hands. Spinning with a spindle, as the Philistines and others did, makes better yarn and goes much faster, but is also much harder to learn.

Materials

Lamb's wool (available in foot care section of many drug stores)

Wooden spoon or stick

Directions

Pull a tuft of wool out of the clump. Loosen it into fibers with your fingers. Pull a few of these fibers partway out of the tuft. With one hand, hold the spot where the fibers join the clump. With the other hand, roll the fibers on your thigh until they twist (spin) into yarn. It is important to keep rolling in the same direction, down or up your thigh. If you roll down and up, it won't work. Try and you'll see.

Add more fibers as you twist, trying to keep about the same amount of fibers coming out of the clump and into the yarn.

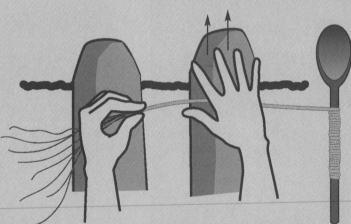

Notice what happens when you stop: the yarn untwists right away. To prevent this, keep rolling until you have several inches twisted, then wrap the twisted part around the spoon handle or stick. Add more fibers to the untwisted end and repeat the rolling and wrapping. Keep spinning until you get tired or run out of wool.

If you keep your yarn wrapped around the stick for several days, it will stay twisted for a while after you unwrap it, but will gradually unwind. To keep yarn twisted, professional spinners twist two or more strands together.

Philistine Language and Writing

Do you like mysteries? Then you'll love the Philistines' language—because nobody knows what it was.

All we know of Philistine speech is a few names, including place-names such as Ashkelon and Ashdod, and kings' names such as Achish (a-KHEESH). Egyptian records give us the names of other Sea Peoples (not all of whom settled in Canaan). These include the Ekwesh, Teresh, Sheklesh, Weshesh, and Sherden. It appears the Sea Peoples liked to say "SH"!

Many scholars guess the Sea Peoples first settling in Canaan spoke languages unrelated to Hebrew, Phoenician, or other Semitic languages. Instead, they guess the Sea Peoples' languages belonged to a language family called Indo-European. This family includes Greek as well as Hittite, a dead language once spoken in Anatolia (ancient Turkey).

Over time, the Philistines and other Sea Peoples seem to have switched to a Semitic language like those used by their new neighbors. Writings from Philistine cities during the late Iron Age use Semitic words. For example, an oil jar from the Philistine city of Ekron bears the label "shemen"—the same word the Israelites used for oil.

The change probably did not happen all at once. People may have continued to hand down their first language to their children. But more and more, the Philistines and other Sea Peoples spoke a language like their neighbors'. Eventually, the languages of the Sea Peoples died out.

ACTIVITY

Mystery Writing

Archaeologists aren't sure if the stamp seals from Ashdod contain early Philistine writing, or any kind of writing at all. Wouldn't you like to baffle archaeologists two thousand years from now? Invent your own alphabet or put together an entirely different system of writing: maybe symbols that stand for syllables or complete words. Carve a mystery message on clay and let it dry, so it will last a long time.

Philistine Writing

One more mystery surrounds the Philistines and the other Sea Peoples: When they first entered Canaan, could they write? Most scholars believe they could. But so far, archaeologists have found no writings that are definitely Philistine. Instead, they've found a couple of "maybes."

Two seals from Ashdod contain mysterious lines that might be writing. Some scholars think the lines look like a kind of writing used in Cyprus during the Bronze Age. No one yet has been able to read the writing from Bronze Age Cyprus, however. So even if this is true, scholars still can't read the seal.

Later in the Iron Age, people living in Philistine cities definitely wrote. By then, they were using a Semitic alphabet. Sometimes they used an alphabet like the Israelites', shaping the letters just a little differently. Other times, they used the Aramaic alphabet.

Archaeologists have found at least one ostracon in every Philistine town or city they have dug up. They have also found inscriptions on storage jars, mostly very short: "dbl" (fig-cake); "kdsh" (holy).

From Ekron comes a longer, fascinating inscription. Read more about it on page 109.

A Philistine might have pressed this seal into moist clay, leaving a mark on the clay. Are the lines on the seal early Philistine writing? Many scholars believe they are.
Courtesy of the Israel Antiquities Authority.

Mystery in a King's Name

During the reigns of two Israelite kings, Saul and Solomon, the Bible mentions a King Achish, ruler of the Philistine city of Gath. Either this ruler Achish lived a *very* long time, or Gath had more than one King Achish.

Hundreds of years later, Assyrian records mention another Philistine king with a similar name, Ikausu (ik-a-OO-soo), ruler of the city Ekron. Scholars have long wondered if Ikausu was just the Assyrians' way of writing Achish. Then, in 1996, an inscription found in Ekron answered their question. Written in a Semitic alphabet around 675 B.C.E., the inscription listed some of Ekron's kings—including a King Achish! Now scholars were sure that King Ikausu of Ekron was the same as Ekron's King Achish. The Assyrians, using a different writing system, just got the name a little off.

But then the scholars wondered: Was Achish really the correct way to write (and pronounce) this king's name? Ancient Semitic writing had no vowels and the same letter (shin or sin) can be pronounced either "SH" or "S." Maybe his name was really a cross between Achish and Ikausu, something like Akhayus (a-KHA-yus).

The scholars liked the idea of the king being named Akhayus. Why? Because in ancient Greek, Akhayus was one way to say "Greek." Maybe this king's name was really King Greek. If so, his name could help resolve another mystery—where the Philistines might have come from.

ACTIVITY

Playing the Name Game

Many scholars think the Sea Peoples gave their names to various places around the eastern Mediterranean. Can you match the correct Sea Peoples with the place that may bear their name? Note that pronunciation and spelling sometimes change over time.

Philistine   Sardinia (island off western Italy)

Sherden   Sicily (large island off southern Italy)

Sikil   Palestine

Did you match Philistine to Palestine? If you did, you're correct. The name "Palestine" comes from "Palaestina," the name used by the Romans after the period covered by this book. "Palaestina," in turn, comes from "Paleshet," the Israelite name for the land of the Philistines. Although "Paleshet" referred to Canaan's southwest coast, "Palaestina" and "Palestine" came to mean a larger area—including the former states of Judah and Israel.

Did you match Sherden to Sardinia, and Sikil to Sicily? Many scholars believe these peoples lived in these islands for some time.

Philistine Work

The Philistines found the coast of Canaan a good place to live and work. It had fertile fields, fair harbors, and access to trade by land and sea.

Like their farmer neighbors, the Philistines also practiced many other kinds of work: building, weaving, trading, producing olive oil and wine, and making tools from bronze and iron. Some historians think the Philistines were the ones who brought skilled ironworking to Canaan.

The Philistines were particularly fine potters. Their clay jugs, pots, bowls, jars, and bottles were far more elegant than those the early Israelites made. Some of their pottery took amazing shapes: fruit, animals, or groups of people. Archaeologists think they used these pottery pieces in religious rituals.

The Philistines painted their pots with animals, plants, or geometric designs in one or two colors. On most two-colored pots, black and brick-red designs stood out against a whitish background. Philistines also made plain pottery in Canaanite styles.

In Ekron, archaeologists found neatly designed kilns (ovens) for baking pottery, with a top part for baking pots and a bottom part for the fire.

Decorated on the front and back with fish and long-necked birds, this Philistine jug has a built-in strainer. Ancient beer and wine often contained bits of solid matter— making a strainer a really good idea. Collection of Israel Antiquities Authority. Exhibit and photo © Israel Museum.

Trade

Two main trade routes crossed Philistine lands. A road called the Way of the Sea headed north from Egypt along the coast. Another route, east to west, was used by traders bringing fragrant Arabian spices. Traders also arrived by ship, docking at Ashkelon and other ports. Philistine merchants traded with people from many different cultures.

The Philistines and their neighbors had no coins or paper money—not because of poverty, but because these things weren't yet used, at least not in their part of the world. The world's first coins appeared in ancient Turkey sometime after 700 B.C.E. It took a while for the idea to spread.

ACTIVITY

Bird-Shaped Bowl

The Philistines made clay bowls with bird heads, wings, and tails attached to them. The bowls may have held food for a god or goddess to "eat" during religious ceremonies. You can make a similar bowl from papier-mâché.

Materials

Newspaper

Aluminum foil, about 2 feet (60 cm)

Masking tape

Paper bowl

Bowl (for mixing papier-mâché)

Measuring cup

Fork

1 cup (240 ml) water

½ cup (120 ml) flour

Acrylic or tempera paint, in brown, white, brick red, and black

Paintbrushes

Jar of water

Directions

Cover the table with some of the newspaper. Tear the rest of the newspaper into strips.

Crumple the foil and shape it into a bird's head with a long neck. Tape the head to the inside of the papu bowl.

Shape more foil into two flat triangular wings and a tail. Tape them to the sides of the bowl.

If the bowl tips, thicken the wings or tail so that it balances.

Mix flour and water in the other bowl. Dip in the newspaper strips, running them between two fingers to remove excess paste. Cover the bird bowl, including the foil parts, with a layer of overlapping strips. Cover with a second layer running crosswise to the first. You don't need to cover the bottom of bowl.

Allow the bowl to dry for several days.

Paint the bowl. Most of the bird bowls were brown, with thin red (and sometimes black) lines in geometric patterns. But feel free to paint it any color you choose.

Instead, the Philistines bought things with bits of silver or gold—usually silver—weighed on scales called balances. Archaeologists have found small bronze pans from these scales in several Philistine cities. To weigh silver, a merchant hung a pan from each end of a pole. Then the merchant put silver chunks in one pan, and weights in the other. Whichever pan was heavier hung lower. The merchant added or removed weights until the pans hung at the same level, then counted the weights to learn the value of the silver.

Along with the balance pans, archaeologists have found different kinds of weights. Most weights were plain, made of bronze or stone, but archaeologists found one shaped like a fish. Philistine merchants used different weights for trade with people from different cultures. Mostly they weighed silver in *shekels* (the way we use pounds or kilograms). But a Phoenician shekel weighed a different amount from an Israelite shekel. Philistine merchants used different weights for both amounts—as well as Egyptian weights called qedets (KEH-dets).

Bird-Loving Philistines

The Philistines often painted their pottery with long-necked birds. They even made some bowls in the shape of birds. In Egyptian pictures, long-necked bird heads decorated the prow and stern of Sea Peoples' ships. What do you think birds might have meant to the Philistines?

ACTIVITY

Merchant's Scale

You can make a nifty-looking scale like those used by Philistine merchants. Israelite, Phoenician, and Mesopotamian merchants used similar scales. Adult supervision recommended.

Materials

Newspaper

2 paper cups

Scissors

Paintbrushes

Acrylic paint, copper-colored or brown

Dowel rod about 15 inches (38 cm) long; ⅜-inch (1 cm) diameter ideal

Sandpaper

Yardstick or tape measure

Pencil

Table for sawing

Phonebooks or other flat heavy objects

Hacksaw

Waxed dental floss or thin string, at least 90 inches (2.3 m) long

2 medium safety pins that will fit around the dowel

Wood clothespin

Pennies

Pebbles

Marker

¼ sheet aluminum foil

Directions

Spread newspaper on the table.

Cut off the upper part of the cups, leaving a 1- to 2-inch (2.5- to 5-cm) rim around the bottom. Discard the upper parts. Set one cup within the other and trim with scissors until they are just about the same size. Separate cups and paint the outsides. Let dry.

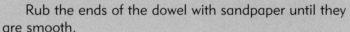

Rub the ends of the dowel with sandpaper until they are smooth.

Measure ½ inch (12 mm) from one end of the dowel. Draw a line as straight as possible all the way around the dowel to mark the spot to be cut. Repeat on the other end.

Lay the dowel on the sawing table with about 3 inches (7.5 cm) of it hanging over the edge. Weigh down the part on the table with heavy objects.

Have an adult carefully cut a shallow notch along the pencil mark with the hacksaw. Have an adult turn the dowel between cuts until there's a groove completely around the dowel. Repeat at the other end of the dowel.

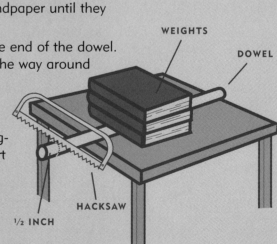

WEIGHTS

DOWEL

HACKSAW

½ INCH

Measure and mark the midpoint between the grooves. Have an adult cut a third shallow groove all around the dowel at this spot.

Cut 6 equal pieces of dental floss, each at least 12 inches (30 cm) long. Set aside the remaining dental floss about 18 inches (45 cm).

When the cups are dry, punch 3 holes spaced equally around the rim of each cup.

Loop a piece of dental floss through a hole in the cup, then through the circle at the bottom of a safety pin (opposite end from the pin's clasp). Tie the dental floss with a square knot.

Repeat this procedure with other pieces of dental floss in the other two holes in the cup, using the same safety pin. Now do the same with the other cup and other pin.

Using another square knot, tie the remaining dental floss (about 18 inches) into a loop. Wrap it several times around the groove in the center of the dowel.

Fasten one safety pin around each edge of the dowel so that the pin rests inside a groove.

Hang the scale from a doorknob. If it tilts to one side, attach the clothespin somewhere along the dowel until it hangs evenly.

Test the scale by putting a penny into each cup. Does it still hang evenly?

Select some pebbles for weights. If you like, mark one with a Phoenician letter *shin* to indicate a shekel. Wrap other smaller pebbles with foil to stand for bits of silver. See if you can measure out a "shekel's" worth of silver.

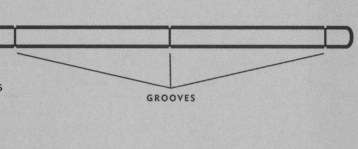

GROOVES

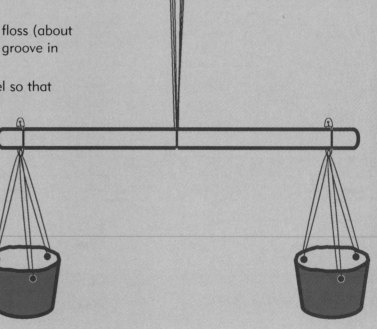

DOORKNOB

Philistine Food

We know about Philistine foods from what they left behind. Archaeologists have found storage jars with the remains of beans, chickpeas, barley, and olives; bones of cattle and other animals; and clay jars that once held beer or wine. They've even found bones from an early Iron-Age hippopotamus, with knife marks showing where the Philistines butchered it for food.

The Philistines probably raised sheep, goats, and cattle for their milk as well as meat; grew wheat as well as barley; and ate figs and grapes. In one ancient garbage dump, archaeologists found bones from at least 12 kinds of fish. (Luckily the fish themselves had rotted long ago— or can you imagine the smell?) Not all Philistine foods resembled their neighbors', however. Pig bones abounded in Philistine ruins. Unlike their neighbors, the Philistines must have eaten a lot of pork.

Onions in Ashkelon

Have you ever heard of a scallion? It's named after the city of Ashkelon. When Romans controlled the area, years after the Iron Age, they called the city "Ascalon" and exported its small green onions. These onions were named after the city they came from. Cookbooks still call for scallions today.

ACTIVITY

Making Philistine Stew

You can make a tasty stew from foods the Philistines ate.
Adult supervision recommended.

Ingredients

½ cup (120 ml) bulgur (available in health food stores)

¾ cup (180 ml) hot water (from tap)

2 scallions

1 tablespoon (15 ml) olive oil

½ teaspoon (8 ml) minced garlic

1 can chickpeas (save liquid)

¼ cup (60 ml) red wine vinegar

½ (8 ml) teaspoon salt

Utensils

Measuring cup

Medium-sized bowl

Saucer or piece of foil

Cutting board

Knife

Measuring spoons

Large frying pan with lid

Spoon

Can opener

Directions

Wash your hands.

Measure bulgur into the bowl.

Pour hot water over the bulgur. Cover the bowl with the saucer or foil.

Rinse the scallions. Chop off the feathery tips and discard. Chop the white and green parts.

Measure oil and pour it into the frying pan. Tip the pan to spread it around. Heat on medium.

Add scallions and garlic to the oil. When they start to sizzle, cook them for two minutes. Stir often.

Turn off the heat and wait a minute until the mixture cools. Add chickpeas and the liquid from the can to the frying pan. Add the vinegar and salt. Add the bulgur and water. Mix well. Turn heat to high. When the stew starts to bubble, lower the heat to medium and cover the pan.

Cook on medium heat for 10 to 15 minutes or until most of the liquid is gone. Stir every few minutes.

Serve hot.

Eating in Ashkelon

Just before the Babylonian King Nebuchadnezzar attacked in 604 B.C.E., Ashkelon was a bustling port city. Archaeologists have unearthed the ruins of a possible wine shop and butcher shop from about that time. In the street outside the wine shop they found a piece of clay inscribed "red wine" and "strong drink." Inside the shop, they found many wine jars, as well as small jugs used to dip out wine for customers' bowls.

Nearby, a butcher shop once held different cuts of meat. Sailors coming off the ships could go to the wine shop for a drink, and residents could buy a haunch of beef in the butcher shop to roast at home.

The Olive-Oil Capital of the Philistines

Under the Assyrians, Ekron became a center for making olive oil. Archaeologists were astounded to find the remains of 115 olive oil presses.

How did the people of Ekron make oil? First, they squashed fresh olives with a stone rolling pin, turning them into paste. Then they added water to the paste. Some of the oil

This is how an oil press from Ekron might have looked when it was new. A press like this squeezes olive oil and juice from baskets full of mashed olives. It takes about 10 hours. Courtesy of Ekron Excavation Project. Drawing by E. Cohen.

A Philistine Cover-up

Have you ever smelled olive oil that's gone bad? It's pretty stinky. People bottling olive oil day after day must have been surrounded by the smell.

To control the odor, the people of Ekron burned incense. Each room for bottling oil held an incense altar. The altars were for religious worship, but the incense also helped mask the smell of rancid (spoiled) oil.

in the paste rose to the top. The workers skimmed it off with tiny clay jugs. This was the finest oil, probably used for cosmetics.

Then the workers scooped the olive paste into straw baskets. They stacked the baskets onto a press—an ancient machine for making olive oil—and topped the stack with a heavy stone. Then they hung weights from the end of a wooden beam jutting out of the wall. The weights pulled the beam heavily onto the

ACTIVITY

Oil and Water

The Philistines separated oil from olive pulp and juice by first mixing it all with water. Then they let everything sit. In time, the oil rose to the top while the water, juice, and bits of olive sank to the bottom.

You can test this yourself. Put ¼ cup (60 ml) of cooking oil into a glass jar. Add ¼ cup (60 ml) of water. Screw on the lid, shake it, then let it sit for a few minutes. What happens? Can you skim off the oil (with a spoon or small scoop) without disturbing the water?

This rebuilt Israelite oil press from the city of Hazor resembles those of the Philistines.
Courtesy of Scott Noegel.

baskets. Oil and olive juice squeezed out through the mesh of the baskets, and dripped into a vat beneath.

After one day, the workers scooped the oily juice from the vat. They added water and let it settle, then poured off the oil. The oil they removed this way was not as fine as the first oil, and was probably used for cooking.

The archaeologists made a model oil press to test how much oil a press like this could produce. They figured that with a good harvest the people of Ekron could have made as much as 290,000 gallons of olive oil in a year. That's an awful lot of olive oil. No doubt the people of Ekron shipped oil to cities all around the area. If they tried to use it all themselves, they would have had a very oily diet.

Philistine Religion

When the Philistines and other Sea Peoples first arrived in Canaan, they worshipped the deities of their home countries. Chief among these was a goddess. We don't know her name, but we do have images they made of her: odd clay statues of a female figure with a face like a bird and a body shaped like a chair.

As the centuries went on, the Philistines may have begun worshipping Canaanite gods. In Ekron, archaeologists have dug up storage jars bearing the words, "dedicated to Asherat." The Canaanites (and some Israelites) worshipped a goddess with a similar name—Asherah. In addition, the Bible says the people of the Philistine city Ashdod worshipped a Canaanite god named Dagon. It also says that Ekron's god was named Baal-zebub. It's quite possible the Philistines worshipped a form of the Canaanite god Baal.

Carved on a stone wall in an Ekron temple about 675 B.C.E. is an inscription. Translated, it says that the ruler of the city, Achish, son of Padi, built the temple for a goddess named Patagiyah. One scholar thinks the end of this name might refer to the Greek mother goddess Gaia (GUY-a). If this is correct, the inscription gives us one more clue that the Philistines came from the Aegean Sea—and tells us that some Philistines never forgot their heritage.

Philistine Worship

The Philistines worshipped their gods and goddesses in temples. These temples were probably used mainly by priests or priestesses; they were too small to hold all the local people at the same time. Altars for sacrificing animals sometimes stood in the courtyard, where the people may have gathered for ceremonies.

Inside most Philistine temples a large raised platform stood along one wall. It probably held an image of the goddess or god, and may have been used for sacrifices. Brick benches lined some of the earlier Philistine temples—perhaps for sitting on, but more likely for displaying offerings.

The early Philistines used special pottery vessels for their worship: drinking cups in the shape of lions' heads; hollow clay tubes shaped into circles and decorated with little animals; and bowls shaped like birds with heads, wings, and tails (see page 113). Some similar objects—lion-headed cups and hollow round clay tubes—were also used in Anatolia and ancient Greece.

We don't know what the Philistines called this goddess. They left statues of her in Ashdod and other settlements.
Collection of Israel Antiquities Authority. Exhibited and photo © Israel Museum.

This model of a lyre-player comes from Ashdod. A lyre is a stringed instrument something like a small harp.
Collection of Israel Antiquities Authority. Exhibited and photo © Israel Museum.

Religious Music

Music was a way for the Philistines to honor their gods and goddesses. A clay model and another piece of pottery from Ashdod showed people playing four instruments: a kind of flute; a flat drum held in the hands; cymbals; and a stringed instrument called a lyre (LIRE, rhyming with wire). These instruments were popular among people of different cultures in the area, including the Israelites.

A Seashell Horn

In one early Philistine temple, archaeologists found another kind of instrument—a trumpet made from a large seashell. The shell—called a conch or triton shell—had the topmost point cut off, leaving a hole. Blowing through the hole made a single musical sound, a deep note that could carry great distances.

Long ago, people from ancient Greece and surrounding areas sometimes made trumpets from these shells. These ancient people may have taught the practice to others living on the coast of Canaan. Perhaps the Philistines brought the horn with them when they moved to Canaan, or perhaps they learned to make it after they arrived in their new home.

Because archaeologists found the shell horn in a temple, they think the Philistines used it in their religious ceremonies. They might have blown it to summon a god.

ACTIVITY

Lyre

With some rubber bands and a couple of box lids, you can make a simple lyre like one the Philistines used.

Materials

Colored markers

Large, strong, shallow rectangular box (the bottom of a chocolate box works well)

Smaller box or lid that fits snugly inside the bottom half of the first box

Scissors

Scotch tape

At least 3 rubber bands of different lengths and thicknesses that fit around the larger box the long way

Pencil

Optional: cardboard (backing from a notepad works well)

Optional: stapler

Directions

Using your colored markers, decorate the inside of the larger box with geometric designs.

Cut a hole or slot in the middle of the smaller box with the scissors

Place the smaller box inside the large box, with the hole facing up. Tape in place. This box will help make the music louder.

Wrap the rubber bands around the larger box the long way. Place the bands closer together at the bottom, and farther apart at the top, so they fan out.

Slide a pencil between the inner box and the strings.

To play, hold your lyre in one hand and twang on the bands with the other. Try moving the pencil around to get different tones.

Some boxes fall apart in time from the pressure of the rubber bands. To prevent this, you can store the rubber bands inside the small box when not playing your lyre. You can also strengthen the edges of the larger box with extra cardboard that has been cut to fit and stapled on.

TAPE

RUBBER BANDS

ACTIVITY

Model Seashell Horn

You can make a model seashell horn that you can really blow. It helps to look at a real seashell while you make this.

Materials

Tiny empty bottle or tube, such as a food coloring bottle or glitter glue container without the plastic spout. Test it first to make sure it makes a good sound. Press the edge of the bottle's mouth firmly against your lower lip and blow hard across the opening.

Tiny piece of aluminum foil

2 ounces Crayola Model Magic

Triton-style shell for model, any size

Directions

Make sure the bottle is empty, clean, and dry. Cover the bottle mouth with a bit of aluminum foil so that the clay won't get inside it.

Study the seashell. Now use Model Magic to form a seashell shape around the bottle. The bottle top should be just at the top of the shell, above the shell's widest part. When the seashell's dry (about 24 hours later), remove the foil—and blow!

This seashell horn comes from a non-Philistine temple in Tel Nami, a Late Bronze Age settlement excavated under the direction of Professor Michal Artzy of the University of Haifa. This horn is much like one found in a Philistine temple in Tel Qasile. Courtesy of Professor Michal Artzy.

Conclusion

Although many people think they were uncultured, the Philistines had a sophisticated civilization. Gradually, however, their culture became more and more like their neighbors'. By the time the Babylonians swept the Philistines into exile, the Philistines lacked a strong identity and their culture did not survive.

Now people remember the Philistines mostly as the Israelites' enemies. Few other traces of their influence survive. One reminder of their power is the name Palestine, which comes from the biblical word for "land of the Philistines."

One of the greatest legacies of the Philistines was their effect on the Israelites. Without the Philistine threat, would the Israelites have demanded a king? Without a king, would the Israelites have built a temple to God? Without the Temple, would the Israelites have maintained their identity and religion? Perhaps, without the Philistines, the Babylonians would have utterly destroyed Israelite culture as well. We might not even have the Bible. Even if we did have a Bible, it would not be the same Bible we have today.

Still, the Philistines and other Sea Peoples were much more than just the Israelites' neighbors. They had their own impressive culture, and brought elegant styles of pottery, city planning, and architecture to Canaan. Under the Assyrians, their cities became centers of commerce and industry. Archaeology has taught us enormous amounts about this busy, creative people. Someday, scholars may solve the mysteries that remain: their language; their writing; and their homeland across the sea.

Epilogue

This book is about the Israelites and their neighbors during the Iron Age—people who lived in a land once called Canaan. Today, modern countries share this region. Their names—Israel, Lebanon, the Palestinian territories—hark back to ancient times, but much history has passed between the Iron Age and today. The countries inhabiting the area now are not the same as the nations of old. Governments and religions have changed. Televisions and computers have replaced parchment and papyrus. "Palestine" no longer means "land of the Philistines," and modern Israel has never had a king.

Not everything has changed since ancient times. Some terrace farms are still in use. Some Lebanese women still make cheese and bread in ways very much like their long-ago ancestors. A few potters and weavers continue old ways of working.

Some of these legacies are dying out. But others are more enduring. Colonies established by the Phoenicians have survived as modern cities. Millions have read the Hebrew Bible. The Israelites' religion has grown and changed and divided, giving rise to Judaism, Christianity, and Islam.

We, too, live in a great civilization. What legacies do we want to leave for the people who follow us?

GLOSSARY

Aegean Sea sea partly bordered by Greece on the west and Turkey on the east

altar surface or platform used for offering sacrifices

amphora large, clay storage container with two handles and a pointed bottom

amulet a charm, usually worn on the body

arc curved line, part of a circle

archaeology study of ancient objects

archaeologist researcher studying the past through excavations

Asherah Canaanite goddess, also worshipped by some Israelites, often associated with trees

asherah tree or pole symbolizing the goddess Asherah

artifact object found in an archaeological excavation, from an earlier time

Aramaean member of dozens of related tribal peoples living in Syria, Assyria, and Babylonia during the Iron Age

Aramaic language or alphabet of the Aramaeans, used by many others during the Iron Age and later; language spoken by Jesus

Assyria ancient country in western Asia between the Tigris and Euphrates rivers, north of Babylonia; part of Mesopotamia

Astarte Canaanite goddess; chief goddess of the Phoenician city-state of Tyre

Baal Canaanite, Phoenician, and Mesopotamian god, associated with storms

Babylonia ancient country in western Asia between the Tigris and Euphrates rivers, south of Assyria; part of Mesopotamia

Babylonian Exile years between 587 B.C.E. and 538 B.C.E., when many Israelites were forced to live in Babylonia

brail rope used to open or close some kinds of sails

Bronze Age period just before the Iron Age, when people made most tools from bronze; years from about 3500 B.C.E. to about 1200 B.C.E.

Canaan name for a region in western Asia during the Bronze Age; today it is divided into Israel, Palestinian territories, Lebanon, and parts of Jordan and Syria

Canaanite person or thing from ancient Canaan, especially during the Bronze Age or earlier

city-state walled city ruled by a king who also controls the surrounding countryside

colony region controlled by a far-away country

courtyard area in the middle of a building, open to the sky

covenant agreement or treaty

cuneiform Mesopotamian writing system using wedges to stand for syllables or words

deity god

Divided Kingdom period when Israel split into a northern kingdom (Israel) and a southern kingdom (Judah)

dynasty series of kings or queens from the same family

El a particular Canaanite god; also, a Semitic word meaning "god," used by many groups, including the Israelites

excavation digging up a spot (a ruin, for example) to study the past

exile being forced to live outside of your home country

exodus leaving a place, especially the Israelites' flight from Egypt

Exodus the second book of the Bible

ferment to turn sugar (such as that in fruit) into alcohol and gas

fibula ancient safety pin

four-room house house with a particular design, common among Israelites and some others during the Iron Age

Egypt country in North Africa along the Nile River

Hebrew Bible record of the Israelite people, including 39 books, sometimes called the Old Testament; holy book of Jews and Christians

hieroglyphs Egyptian writing system using pictures for words, consonants, or groups of consonants

high place hilltop where Israelites worshipped

hull body of a ship or boat

ingot chunk of shaped metal used in trade

inscription words which are written, carved, or engraved

Iron Age period following the Bronze Age, when people began making some good-quality tools from iron; years from about 1200 B.C.E. to 587 B.C.E.

Israel country in western Asia during the Iron Age (United Monarchy period); also, the kingdom north of Judah during the Divided Kingdom period; also, a modern country in about the same location

Israelite person or thing belonging to one of twelve tribes who occupied Canaan's southern hill country at the start of the Iron Age; also, person or thing from the northern kingdom during the Divided Kingdom period; in this book, a person or thing from either the northern or southern kingdom during the Divided Kingdom

Israeli citizen of the modern state of Israel

Jerusalem ancient capital of Israel established by King David; today, a city holy to Jews, Christians, and Muslims

Judah the kingdom south of Israel during the Divided Kingdom period

kiln oven for baking clay pottery

kilt skirt worn by men or boys

Lebanon ancient and modern country north of Israel on the Mediterranean coast

Levite member of the Israelite tribe of Levi, assistant to Israelite priest

lyre stringed musical instrument

Mediterranean Sea large body of water bordered by southern Europe, western Asia and northern Africa

Melqart chief god of the Phoenician city-state Tyre

Mesopotamia region in western Asia between the Tigris and Euphrates rivers, an area today that is mostly in Iraq

monarchy kingdom

mordant chemical that helps dye attach to the fabric so it doesn't wash out

observant following the laws and customs of a religion

Old Testament the Hebrew Bible; the part of the Christian Bible before Jesus

ostracon potsherd with writing on it

Palestine From 1918–1948, the name used for the land between the Jordan River and the Mediterranean Sea, ruled then by the British and historically called Eretz Israel by Jews; from 1948, this land was divided among the State of Israel, the Gaza Strip (ruled by Egypt) and the West Bank (incorporated into the Hashemite Kingdom of Jordan)

Palestinian territories The land conquered by Israel in the 1967 War, including the West Bank (which had been part of Jordan) and the Gaza Strip (which had been administered by Egypt); in the 1990s, Israel began transferring parts of this land to the new Palestine Authority, which governs them alone or jointly with Israel

papyrus mashed stems of a plant, pressed into a material like paper and used to write on

parchment tanned animal skin used to write on

people more than one person; also, all those sharing the same religion, government, or culture

pharaoh ancient Egyptian ruler

Philistia land inhabited by the Philistines during the Iron Age

Philistine person or thing belonging to the Philistines, an Iron-Age people living in the western part of the country now called Israel; also, a person who lacks culture or appreciation for the arts

Phoenicia group of city-states in the northern part of Canaan, bordering the Mediterranean Sea, during the Iron Age

Phoenician a Canaanite living in Phoenicia during the Iron Age

pillared house house where pillars replace one or two walls

potsherd piece of broken clay pot

press machine that squeezes oil from olives or juice from grapes

prophet to the Israelites, a holy person who could voice God's wishes and sometimes predict the future

prow front part of a boat or ship

Quran Muslim holy book

Sabbath a day of each week set aside for prayer and rest

Samaria capital of the northern kingdom of Israel during the Divided Kingdom period

Sea Peoples a number of groups, including the Philistines, who attacked Egypt from land and sea shortly before 1175 B.C.E., some of them settling in Canaan

Semitic a group of related languages including Hebrew, Phoenician, Arabic, and Aramaic

shekel unit of weight in the ancient Near East; also, a shekel's weight of silver or gold

sandalwood fragrant wood used in perfumes and incense

seal object that makes a picture or words when pressed into moist clay

Sherden one of the Sea Peoples who settled in Canaan

Sikils one of the Sea Peoples who settled in Canaan

spindle hand tool for making thread or yarn

stern back of a boat or ship

Syria country northeast of ancient Israel and north of Lebanon in ancient times; also, a modern country in a similar location

terrace farming method of creating flat fields on a hillside

tophet burial ground for babies sacrificed to a god or goddess

tribute payment of precious goods from one ruler or country to another

tunic garment like a long shirt

Tyre Phoenician city-state

United Monarchy period in Israelite history when a single king ruled the entire land, before Israel split into northern and southern kingdoms

ACKNOWLEDGMENTS

I am extremely grateful to the many people who helped with this book.

First and foremost, I thank Scott Noegel, Ph.D., Professor of Biblical and Ancient Near Eastern Studies at the University of Washington, for his insightful review of the manuscript, answers to my many questions, and the loan of his slides. I'm also grateful to other experts for generously reviewing parts of my drafts: Oded Borowski, Ph.D., Associate Professor of Biblical Archaeology and Hebrew and Director of Mediterranean Archaeology at Emory University; Seymour Gitin, Ph.D., Dorot Director and Professor of Archaeology, W. F. Albright Institute of Archaeological Research in Jerusalem; Ann E. Killebrew, Ph.D., Assistant Professor (Archaeology of the Levant), Pennsylvania State University; Glenn Markoe, Ph.D., Curator of Classical and Near Eastern Art, Cincinnati Art Museum; and Jeremy Alk, MA, Jewish educator. In addition, I'd like to thank Gloria London, Ph.D., of the University of Washington's Burke Museum, for her generous assistance with resources. Any errors are my own.

I am utterly grateful to the children who helped, particularly Leora Alk, Rebekah Liebermann, and Bronwyn Romannose, who tested projects with me for more than a year. I also thank Aleph Cervo, Nathan LaSala, Palma London, Nelly Nicklason, Coby Vardy, nine children from P'ri Eitz Or Sunday School, and the fourth and fifth grade classes (2000–2001) of the Jewish Day School of Metropolitan Seattle.

I'm grateful to the many adults who read drafts or helped refine activities: Michael Almoslino, Ann Davidge, Miriam Driss, Frannie Ein, Arlene Goldbard, Linda Harris, Pat Richmond, Stephanie Rubin, Tracy Salter, Reed Sutherland, and members of my critique group. Special thanks to Josée Perez, the Jewish Day School's extraordinary art teacher, for arranging my work with students and for her creative ideas.

My gratitude to those who provided key insights, facts, and connections: Inbar Baruch from the University of Haifa; Julia Ceffalo and others from Seattle's Weaving Works; Douglas Clark, Ph.D., Professor of Biblical Studies and Archaeology at Walla Walla College and Co-director of the Madaba Plains Project in Jordan; Huda Giddens; Saeedeh P. Jamshidi; Carol Meyers, Ph.D., Professor of Biblical Studies and Archaeology at Duke University; Joel Migdal, Ph. D., Professor of International Studies at the University of Washington; Kim Rolling; Brannon Wheeler, Ph.D., Associate Professor of Islamic Studies and Chair of Comparative Religion at the University of Washington; and Andro Wipplinger from Earthues.

For research help, I thank the wonderful staff at the Seattle Public Library's Northeast branch, and Monica Blanchard of Catholic University. For help with the art, I am grateful to Jane Gerler, Suzanne Krom, Chris Madell of the American Schools of Oriental Research, Caren Monasterski, and Sis Polin.

I give special thanks to my agent, Marian Reiner, and Cynthia Sherry and my editor Jerome Pohlen of Chicago Review Press. Finally, my gratitude to Beth, Sara, Laurie, Michael, Gail, and Lynn, for their support.

CHILDREN'S BOOKS AND WEB SITES FOR FURTHER INVESTIGATIONS

Books

Ballard, Robert D. *The Lost Wreck of the Isis.* New York: Scholastic Inc., 1990.

Broida, Marian. *Ancient Egyptians and Their Neighbors: An Activity Guide.* Chicago: Chicago Review Press, 1999.

Gonen, Rivka. *Fired Up! Making Pottery in Ancient Times.* Minneapolis: Runestone Press, 1993.

Sanders, Nancy I. *Old Testament Days: An Activity Guide.* Chicago: Chicago Review Press, 1999.

Tubb, Jonathan N. *Eyewitness Books: Bible Lands.* New York: Alfred A. Knopf, 1991.

Web Sites

American Schools of Oriental Research: Outreach
www.asor.org/outreach

Archaeological Adventure
library.thinkquest.org/3011/home.htm

Archaeological Institute of America
www.archaeological.org

British Museum: Young Friends
www.thebritishmuseum.ac.uk/join/youngfriends/index.html

Hebrew University of Jerusalem: Jerusalem Mosaic
jeru.huji.ac.il

Israel Antiquities Authority: Youth
www.israntique.org.il/eng/yutext.html

Israel Museum: Archaeology
www.imj.org.il/archaeology

Metropolitan Museum of Art
www.metmuseum.org

Michael C. Carlos Museum of Emory University: Odyssey Online
carlos.emory.edu/ODYSSEY

NOVA On Line-Be an Archaeologist
www.pbs.org/wgbh/nova/laventa/archaeologist.html

Oriental Institute, University of Chicago
www-oi.uchicago.edu/OI

Semitic Museum, Harvard University
www.fas.harvard.edu/~semitic

University of Pennsylvania Museum of Archaeology and Anthropology
www.upenn.edu/museum

Canaan and Ancient Israel
www.museum.upenn.edu/Canaan/index.html

Excavation Web Sites

Ashkelon
www.fas.harvard.edu/~semitic/ashkelon_dig.html

Beirut
www.lebanon.com/construction/beirut/arche.htm

Hazor
unixware.mscc.huji.ac.il/~hatsor/hazor.html

Madaba Plains
www.wwc.edu/mpp

Megiddo
www.tau.ac.il/~archpubs/megiddo/index.html

Tel Dor
www.arts.cornell.edu/jrz3/TelDor/Dor-Main.html

BIBLIOGRAPHY

General

Ben-Tor, Amnon, ed. *The Archaeology of Ancient Israel*, translated by R. Greenberg. New Haven: Yale University Press and Tel Aviv: The Open University of Israel, 1992.

Healey, John. *The Early Alphabet*. London: The Trustees of the British Museum, 1990.

London, Gloria and Douglas Clark, eds. *Ancient Ammonites and Modern Arabs*. Amman, Jordan: American Center of Oriental Research, 1997.

Mazar, Amihai. *Archaeology of the Land of the Bible, 10,000–586 B.C.E.* New York: Doubleday, 1990.

Schoville, Keith. "Canaanites and Amorites." In Alfred Hoerth et al., eds., *Peoples of the Old Testament World*. Grand Rapids, MI: Baker Books, 1994, pp. 157–182.

Stern, Ephraim. *Archaeology of the Land of the Bible, Volume II: The Assyrian, Babylonian, and Persian Periods (732–332 B.C.E.)*. New York: Doubleday, 2001.

Tubb, Jonathan N. *Canaanites*. Norman, OK: University of Oklahoma Press, 1998.

Whitt, William D. "The Story of the Semitic Alphabet." In Jack Sasson et al., eds., *Civilizations of the Ancient Near East*. New York: Charles Scribner's Sons, 1995, pp. 2379–2397.

Israelites

Beer, Moshe. "Judaism (Babylonian)," translated by Menahem Erez. In David Noel Freedman et al., eds., *Anchor Bible Dictionary, Volume III*. New York: Doubleday, 1992, pp. 1076–1083.

Biran, Avraham. *Biblical Dan*. Jerusalem: Israel Exploration Society, 1994.

Borowski, Oded. *Agriculture in Iron Age Israel*. Winona Lake, IN: Eisenbrauns, 1987.

Borowski, Oded. *Every Living Thing: Daily Use of Animals in Ancient Israel*. London: AltaMira Press, 1997.

Borowski, Oded. "Eat, Drink, and Be Merry: The Ancient Mediterranean Diet." Paper given at American Schools of Oriental Research Annual Meeting, Nashville, TN. November 15–18, 2000.

Cahill, Jane, Karl Reinhard, David Tarler, and Peter Warnock. "Scientists Examine Remains of Ancient Bathroom." *Biblical Archaeology Review* 17, May/June 1991, pp. 64–69.

Caudet, Annie. "Art and Architecture in Canaan and Ancient Israel." In Jack Sasson et al., eds., *Civilizations of the Ancient Near East*. New York: Charles Scribner's Sons, 1995, pp. 2671–2691.

Dever, William G. "Palaces and Temples in Canaan and Ancient Israel." In Jack Sasson et al., eds., *Civilizations of the Ancient Near East*. New York: Charles Scribner's Sons, 1995, pp. 605–614.

Edelstein, Gershon and Shimon Gibson. "Ancient Jerusalem's Rural Food Basket." *Biblical Archaeology Review* 8, July/Aug. 1982, pp. 46–54.

Finkelstein, Israel. *The Archaeology of the Israelite Settlement*. Jerusalem: Israel Exploration Society, 1988.

Gruber, Mayer I. "Private Life in Canaan and Ancient Israel." In Jack Sasson et al., eds., *Civilizations of the Ancient Near East*. New York: Charles Scribner's Sons, 1995, pp. 633–648.

Henshaw, Richard. *Female and Male: The Cultic Personnel*. Allison Park, PA: Pickwick Publications, 1994.

Herr, Larry and Douglas Clark. "Excavating the Tribe of Reuben." *Biblical Archaeology Review* 27, March/April 2001, pp. 36–47, 64, 66.

Holladay, John S. Jr. "House, Israelite." In David Noel Freedman et al., eds., *Anchor Bible Dictionary, Volume III*. New York: Doubleday, 1992, pp. 308–318.

Isserlin, B.S.J. *The Israelites*. London: Thames and Hudson, 1998.

Lemche, Niels Peter. "The History of Ancient Syria and Palestine: An Overview." In Jack Sasson et al., eds., *Civilizations of the Ancient Near East*. New York: Charles Scribner's Sons, 1995, pp. 1195–1218.

Mazar, Amihai. "The 'Bull Site'—An Iron Age I Open Cult Place." *Bulletin of the American Schools of Oriental Research* #246, 1982, pp. 27–42.

Meyer, Carol, and Susan Ackerman. "The World of Women: Gender and Archaeology." Papers given at American Schools of Oriental Research Annual Meeting, Nashville, TN. November 15–18, 2000.

Naveh, Joseph. *Early History of the Alphabet*. Jerusalem: The Magnes Press, Hebrew University, 1982.

Niditch, Susan. *Ancient Israelite Religion*. New York: Oxford University Press, 1997.

Perdue, Leo G., Joseph Blenkinsopp, John J. Collins, and Carol Meyers. *Families in Ancient Israel*. Louisville, KY: Westminster John Knox Press, 1997.

Pritchard, James B., ed. *Ancient Near Eastern Texts Relating to the Old Testament,* 2nd ed. Princeton, NJ: Princeton University Press, 1955, p. 321.

Seger, Karen, ed. *Portrait of a Palestinian Village: The Photographs of Hilma Granqvist*. London: The Third World Centre for Research and Publishing, 1981.

Stager, Lawrence E. "The Archaeology of the Family in Ancient Israel." *Bulletin of the American Schools of Oriental Research* 260, November 1985, pp. 1–35.

Stern, Ephraim, ed. *The New Encyclopedia of Archaeological Excavations in the Holy Land*. New York: Simon & Shuster, 1993.

Editors of Time-Life Books. *The Holy Land*. Alexandria, VA: Time-Life Books, 1992.

Zevit, Ziony. *The Religions of Ancient Israel: A Synthesis of Parallactic Approaches.* New York: Continuum, 2001.

Phoenicians

Albenda, Pauline. "Western Asiatic Women in the Iron Age: Their Image Revealed." *Biblical Archaeologist* 46, Spring 1983, pp. 82–88.

Bartoloni, Piero. "Ships and Navigation" and "Commerce and Industry." In Moscati, Sabatino, ed., *The Phoenicians*. New York: Rizzoli International Publications, Inc., 1999, 84–100.

Bondi, Sandro Filippo. "City Planning and Architecture." In Moscati, Sabatino, ed., *The Phoenicians*. New York: Rizzoli International Publications, Inc., 1999, pp. 311–348.

Casson, Lionel. *Ships and Seafaring in Ancient Times*. Austin: University of Texas Press, 1994.

Ciasca, Antonia. "Masks and Protomes." In Moscati, Sabatino, ed., *The Phoenicians*. New York: Rizzoli International Publications, Inc., 1999, pp. 406–417.

Edey, Maitland A. *The Sea Traders*. New York: Time-Life Books, 1974.

Garbini, Giovanni. "The Question of the Alphabet." In Moscati, Sabatino, ed., *The Phoenicians.* New York: Rizzoli International Publications, Inc., 1999, pp. 101–119.

Harden, Donald. *The Phoenicians*. New York: Frederick A. Praeger, 1962.

Markoe, Glenn E. *Phoenicians.* Los Angeles: University of California Press, 2000.

Moscati, Sabatino. "A Civilization Rediscovered," "Arts and Crafts," and "Metal Bowls." In Moscati, Sabatino, ed., *The Phoenicians*. New York: Rizzoli International Publications, Inc., 1999, pp. 8–16, 306–310, 491–499.

Pliny. *Natural History, Volume VIII*, translated by W. H. S. Jones. Cambridge, MA: Harvard University Press, 1963, pp. 435–437.

The Jewish Publication Society. *JPS Hebrew-English Tanakh.* Philadelphia: The Jewish Publication Society, 2000.

Wilford, John. "Finds in Egypt Date Alphabet in Earlier Era." *New York Times*, November 14, 1999, pp. A1, A16.

Zeiderman, I. Irving. "Seashells and Ancient Purple Dyeing." *Biblical Archaeologist* 53, June 1990, pp. 98–101.

Philistines

Baruch, Inbar. "Triton Shells from the Eastern Mediterranean and Their Cultic Use During the Late Bronze Age." paper given at American Schools of Oriental Research Annual Meeting, November 2000.

Dothan, M. and Y. Porath. *Ashdod IV: Excavation of Area M.* 'Atiqot. Jerusalem: Israel Ministry of Education and Culture, Hebrew University, and Israel Exploration Society, 1982.

Dothan, Trude. "Ekron of the Philistines: Part I: Where They Came From, How They Settled Down and the Place They Worshiped In." *Biblical Archaeology Review* 16, Jan/Feb. 1990, pp. 26–36.

Dothan, Trude. "Initial Philistine Settlement: From Migration to Coexistence." In Seymour Gitin, Amihai Mazar and Ephraim Stern, eds., *Mediterranean Peoples in Transition.* Jerusalem: Israel Exploration Society, 1998, pp. 148–161.

Dothan, Trude. *The Philistines and their Material Culture.* New Haven: Yale University Press, 1982.

Dothan, Trude. "Tel Miqne-Ekron: An Iron Age I Philistine Settlement in Canaan." In Silberman, Neil A. and Small, David B., eds., *The Archaeology of Israel.* Sheffield, Great Britain: Sheffield Academic Press, 1997, pp. 96–106.

Dothan, Trude and Moshe Dothan. *People of the Sea.* New York: Macmillan Publishing Company, 1992.

Dothan, Trude and Seymour Gitin. "Ekron of the Philistines: How They Lived, Worked and Worshiped for Five Hundred Years." *Biblical Archaeology Review* 16, Jan/Feb. 1990, pp. 20–25.

Ehrlich, Carl S. *The Philistines in Transition.* New York: E.J. Brill, 1996.

Gitin, Seymour. "Ekron of the Philistines: Part II: Olive-Oil Suppliers to the World." *Biblical Archaeology Review* 16, March/April 1990, pp. 33–42, 59.

Gitin, Seymour. "The Last Days of the Philistines." *Archaeology* 45, May 1992, pp. 26–31.

Gitin, Seymour, Trude Dothan, and Joseph Naveh. "A Royal Dedicatory Inscription from Ekron." *Israel Exploration Journal* 47, No. 1–2, 1997, pp. 1–16.

Gore, Rick. "Samson, Goliath, Herod, Alexander, Richard the Lion-Hearted May Have Walked the Streets of Ashkelon, Ancient City of the Sea." *National Geographic* 199, January 2001, pp. 66–93.

Karageorghis, Vassos. "Hearths and Bathtubs in Cyprus: A 'Sea Peoples' Innovation?" In Seymour Gitin, Amihai Mazar, and Ephraim Stern, eds., *Mediterranean Peoples in Transition*. Jerusalem: Israel Exploration Society, 1998, pp. 276–282.

Killebrew, Ann E. "Aegean-Style Early Philistine Pottery in Canaan During the Iron I Age: A Stylistic Analysis of Mycenaean IIC:1b Pottery and Its Associated Wares." In Oren, Eliezer D., ed., *The Sea Peoples and Their World: A Reassessment.* Philadelphia: The University Museum, University of Pennsylvania, 2000, pp. 233–253.

Killebrew, Ann E. "Pottery Kilns from Deir el-Balah and Tel Miqne-Ekron." In Seger, Joe, ed., *Retrieving the Past*. Winona Lake, Indiana: Published for the Cobb Institute of Archaeology and distributed by Eisenbrauns, 1996, pp. 135–162.

Lichtheim, Miriam. *Ancient Egyptian Literature, Volume II*. Berkeley, CA: University of California Press, 1976, pp. 224–229.

Mazar, Amihai. *Excavations at Tell Qasile, Part I*. Jerusalem: The Institute of Archaeology, 1980.

Mazar, Amihai. *Excavations at Tell Qasile, Part II*. Jerusalem: The Institute of Archaeology, 1985.

Naveh, Joseph. "Writing and Scripts in Seventh-Century B.C.E. Philistia: The New Evidence from Tell Jemmeh." *Israel Exploration Journal* 35, 1985, pp. 8–21.

Singer, Itamar. "How Did the Philistines Enter Canaan? A Rejoinder." *Biblical Archaeology Review* 18, Nov/Dec. 1992, pp. 44–46.

Stager, Lawrence E. "The Fury of Babylon: Ashkelon and the Archaeology of Destruction." *Biblical Archaeology Review* 22, Jan/Feb. 1996, pp. 56–69, 76–77.

Steiglitz, Robert R. "Did the Philistines Write?" *Biblical Archaeology Review* 8, July/Aug. 1982, p. 31.

Wood, Bryant G. "The Philistines Enter Canaan—Were they Egyptian Lackeys or Invading Conquerors?" *Biblical Archaeology Review* 17, Nov/Dec. 1991, pp. 44–52, 89.

INDEX